The Mad Wor
Village Postman

by Stephen James

Copyright © 2021 Stephen James

ISBN: 9798737887506

All rights reserved, including the right to reproduce this book, or portions thereof in any form. No part of this text may be reproduced, transmitted, downloaded, decompiled, reverse engineered, or stored, in any form or introduced into any information storage and retrieval system, in any form or by any means, whether electronic or mechanical without the express written permission of the author.

The illustration on the front cover of this book was done by David Dudley.

www.totalpencilportraits.co.uk

The Author

Stephen is a retired postman who lives with his wife, Jayne. They have been together for 32 years now but only married 2 years ago as it took a long time to decide. He is a keen motorcyclist and also has a liking for the wonderful motorcars manufactured by Rolls-Royce and Bentley. The family consists of George, the cat, Bentley the chocolate Labrador and Royce who is a yellow Labrador. Both dogs are P.A.T., (Pets as Therapy) dogs although Stephen doesn't always find this to be the case.

This book is for my lovely wife Jayne.
Living with me has turned her grey.

INTRODUCTION

When I got my first computer, it coincided with having less and less time to stand on doorsteps chatting with customers and friends on my rural delivery. So, we started communicating by email. One day in early 2006, I had a couple of things I thought worthy of sharing so I wrote an email, referring to these two situations as 'Mad World 1' and 'Mad World 2.' The recipients encouraged me to write more, so I did. Over the following 10-15 years, Mad World emails were written and shared as and when I had something I thought worth sharing. This book is not all about my day job. It includes experiences from my private life, my hobbies and vehicles, and my wife's job at the time, working for Post Office Counters. You will also read about some of the things I have done with my Rolls-Royce and Bentley motorcars. Everything is taken from real-life events but has, of course, been written from my point of view. I have always tried to see the funny side of things. Other people may have a different opinion about those same events and I do respect that.

What started as Mad World 1 & 2 grew to a volume of work that I was encouraged to share with a wider audience. The tales are in no particular order other than that in which they were written. I have left the format as it has always been as I think it reads better that way.

Emails aren't the answer for every kind of writing and I think it is important to remember just how much people enjoy receiving a hand-written card or letter. We should all try and write a letter or send a card from time to time to keep our great postal service doing what it has done for generations, keeping people connected.

The English language is a wonderful thing and I enjoy the fun that can be had when using it. I hope you enjoy the collection of experiences and observations that I have included in this book.

Welcome to my Mad World.

Stephen James.

MAD WORLD PART 1

The two ladies I took to the registry office last week wore trousers.

This week it is to be a conventional wedding and the bride and groom will both be in skirts.

And I thought I had some funny habits!

MAD WORLD PART 2

We have 2 part timers starting at work over the next two weeks and they will be on town rounds. This will mean that the chap who was the last in and is thus the junior member of our team, will have to be moved on to another round. This is something he is very much against. This morning he was very vocal on the subject and stated that the rules are that all the rounds have to be re-picked. This is, of course, untrue. However, what gives me the biggest laugh is:

As the junior member of our team he would get the last pick anyway.

MAD WORLD 3
THE CHIROPRACTOR

On Tuesday of this week, a colleague of mine could hardly walk. He was experiencing terrific pain down his left leg. He said he was really worried as he didn't think it was muscular so it could be nerve pain. Sciatica perhaps? I told him that if it were nerve pain, that would keep him awake at night. Apparently it had. So, I suggested he ought to get it looked at. He was in sufficient pain to actually take the details off me for my osteopath. Mind you, experience has proved that nine out of ten people who've had my osteopath's details off me never actually go.

Today his walking was a bit better. The painkillers seemed to be working. He told me that he'd bumped into a customer of his yesterday who is a chiropractor. He had told her of his problem, and she persuaded him to make an appointment to see her the next afternoon, on Thursday. My colleague did tell me he would keep my chap's details in case this didn't work but, at least the chiropractor was local. I had also noticed that the chiropractor was a woman.

I told my colleague that he should make sure he was wearing clean underpants for the treatment. About ten minutes later he stopped laughing. I had to convince him that, although we often joke about these things, I was in fact being deadly serious this time. I had to explain to him, as he had never been to anything other than a GP before, that osteopaths and chiropractors work on you in your underwear so that they can see what is going on with your back. The things my own osteopath can work out by watching someone bend forward, back, and to the side, are simply incredible. And now the fun started.

I told my colleague that when the chiropractor lady tells him to undress down to his underpants, for goodness' sake don't start giggling like he had just now because she'll think: 'I've got a right one here, he's getting all giggly because he's got to take his clothes off in front of me.'

Once my colleague had composed himself again, he gave it some more thought and then said: "Steve, what do I do if I start stripping off and she starts stripping off as well?" "For Christ's sake, make me an appointment for Friday", that's what.

MAD WORLD 4
IT'S COMMON SENSE

We had the usual splitting up of a round this morning and one colleague, upon hearing who was getting Upper Lake, said: "Why don't I do Upper Lake as I often do when you're splitting up the High Street? That's the trouble here, no common sense any more in this office."

The PHG (Postman Higher Grade, as they were once called) said: "That's a good idea, why didn't I think of that?"

Colleague went on to say, "Funny how we aren't Management and yet we can do a better job of splitting the rounds up."

Well, I must say, I was keeping quiet throughout this exchange but I did think he was doing rather well.

PHG, wanting to change the subject rapidly as he was losing the argument here, asked the same colleague: "How did you get on last night at the White Rock Theatre?"

Colleague replied: "It wasn't last night, it's tonight."

PHG: "But I thought you had tickets for the 21st?"

Colleague: "Yes, my tickets are for the 21st, so I'm going tonight."

PHG: "Today is the 22nd, last night was the 21st."

Me: "What was that you were saying just now about no common sense in the office?"

.

MAD WORLD 5
NEED A NEW JOB

Having worked in Management in my last job, I've seen interviews from both sides of the table. As an interviewee, I thought the main aim had to be to at least get offered the job and then decide if you want it. With the current unrest in the office, there is the usual round of job applications and occasional interviews going on, and a couple of my colleagues were previously motor mechanics. One of them is looking to get back into that line of work but doesn't fancy a modern workshop as he isn't computer-literate. Last Saturday, he started asking me about Sargeants of Goudhurst as they have advertised for a mechanic to train in the service and restoration of Rolls-Royce and Bentley motorcars. He has an interview today, Tuesday. Yesterday I asked him if he has certificates to show he knows which way round to hold a spanner. He said he has and they must be in the house somewhere. I thought he would have spent Sunday looking for them, but never mind.

So, today he is all set to go to that Rolls-Royce temple of worship in Goudhurst in the hopes of finding a route out of his current job. This morning I wished him luck and suggested he mustn't be late and should look smart.

He said: "Don't worry, I think this is the direction I want to be going in and could be just the sort of job I am looking for."

I said: "But you also need to be just the chap they are looking for."

He said: "Oh, I hadn't thought of it like that."

Silly me! I hadn't realised how honoured we have been by his presence these past few years.

MAD WORLD 6
HASTINGS ROBBERY

Talking of Rolls-Royce and Bentley, when the great Hastings money house was robbed a few years ago, it coincided with me arriving at Rolls club events with the Corniche and the Silver Shadow. Some of the other members thought it good sport to pull my leg that the only clue the police had to go on was that one of the robbers was seen to have ginger eye brows under his balaclava. Now, we've had 50 million quid nicked and there have been two photo-fit pictures on the television and one chap has a peaked cap and a ginger beard.

I'm sticking with the woolly hat from now on.

MAD WORLD 7
FINGERLESS GLOVES

As you all know, my employer invests huge resources in to ensuring my health, wealth and happiness. During the winter time I am, if I'm lucky, provided with company issue gloves to keep my pinkies warm. Whilst delivering to one of my elderly and, as I thought more intellectual customers, he remarked on my fingerless gloves.

He said: "I have never seen anything like those before, what a good idea. Did you just get an ordinary pair of gloves and cut the fingers off?"

I just looked at him in disbelief for a moment and then, never being one to miss an opportunity, I held my fingerless gloved hand up in front of him and gave him my answer:

"No John, it's just another sign of company cutbacks."

MAD WORLD 8
77 YEAR OLD LEARNER DRIVER

I know we all have elderly relatives and I wouldn't want to cause offence to anyone. However, I was amazed to learn that a lady went to the counter in our local Post Office the other day and passed her application form for her first provisional driving licence through to be checked. It was all filled in correctly and had a good likeness photo attached. Date of Birth: 1928. Yes, she is going to learn to drive at the age of 77. I hope she finds a driving instructor with a sense of humour.

MAD WORLD 9
SHOPPING AT BOOTS

I've never been fortunate enough to have to fight women off so I had no experience of such matters until a recent trip to the Boots branch near to where I work.

I selected the item I wished to purchase and proceeded to the checkout to pay. There were, as usual, one or two ladies serving behind the counter. When it was my turn to be served, the assistant held her hand out to take my intended purchase along with the money to pay.

"Ooh, laddie," she said, with a broad Scottish accent, "What a beautiful beard you have. It really is super."

"Thank you." I replied.

She turned to put the money in the till whilst going on to say: "My Son is trying to grow a beard but he is only 19 and it isn't a patch on yours."

"Well it takes a bit of time." I replied. What the hell else could I say? My knees were already knocking.

She gave me my purchase and I held my hand out for my change.

She held my hand tight as she said: "That really is such a lovely, lovely beard." I don't recall if she actually let go of me or I just managed to escape, but I've never been back.

MAD WORLD 10
THE DREADED ITCH

The next time I needed to purchase something from Boots I thought it would be wise to visit a bigger branch. I was suffering from a problem I've had all my life, namely, dry skin. Some ordinary bath products seem to make it worse and can cause my skin to really itch. An itchy arm or leg isn't too embarrassing but, hey, this had got out of hand. There are some places you don't want to be scratching when you are out on the street. The best product I've ever had was Boots Moisturising Crème Bath. I was on a mission to find a bottle if they were still making it.

I searched up and down all the aisles and couldn't find the bubble bath products anywhere. As I was quite desperate, I decided to queue at the counter and ask for assistance. When I got to the front of the queue the assistant asked me: "Can I help you?"

"I hope so," I replied, "Do you still do a product called Boots Moisturising Crème Bath?"

"All our bath products are upstairs," she told me. 'Why didn't I think of that?' I thought as I climbed the stairs.

All I needed was one bottle. What I found was a counter about 30ft long and 6 shelves deep all full of bath products. They had bottles of stuff that could do just about anything for you. In fact some of the things the bottles were supposed to be able to do for you I'd always thought you had to go abroad for! I read the labels and tried to make a decision but I couldn't find the exact product that I had been looking for. I thought I'd get an assistant to advise me instead. She was extremely helpful and gave me one or two choices which were different from what I'd originally thought of and then left me to deliberate for a bit longer. I finally decided on a bottle of Boots Oil of Evening Primrose with Vitamin E Moisturising 'Crème' Bath. I was attracted by the Vitamin E as I often use Vitamin E cream for cuts on my hands and things. The bottle also stated that it would give my skin a natural radiance, by Jove.

I took the bottle to the counter to pay and felt really pleased that the decision had been made. The same lady who had advised me was now serving at the till and took the bottle and scanned it, as they do, while I got the money out to pay. I really was that close. How could it possibly go wrong? Why does it always happen to me? The slight delay while I was trying to reach my money [short arms, deep pockets] enabled the assistant to read the label.

"You don't want this one," she said.

"Yes I do," I replied.

"But this one isn't very manly," she went on.

"I'm not worried about how manly it is," I said, "I just want one that does the job."

"But you don't want to go around smelling like this." she protested.

"I really don't mind what I smell like as long as I don't itch," I replied.

By now people were starting to stare. I'm understandably uncomfortable with people looking at me when someone is going on about my not being very manly and how I shouldn't smell a certain way.

The assistant unscrewed the cap and shoved the bottle under my nose.

"But you can't go around smelling like this," she said.

Well, I'm sorry to say that I started to lose my cool.

"OK, but if you don't think I should have that one then you jolly well go over there and find me the one you think I should have." I told her.

Off she went and back she came, 2 bottles in hand.

"This is what you want and its buy one get one free." she said.

Great. So now if I have a bath and don't get on with it I will have two bottles that are no use to me instead of one.

MAD WORLD 11
WRONG DAY FOR WORK

Two of the chaps I work with live in the Eastbourne/Hailsham area and so one of them collects the other on the way to work and they travel in together.

On Monday morning this week, the chap from Hailsham was woken up by the noise his cat was making, because the cat wanted the door opened. The chap looked at the clock and, seeing it was 3.15am, switched his alarm clock off and got up. After sorting the cat out, he got washed and dressed. As he put his coat on to await his lift, he glanced at the clock to see how he was doing for time. It was now 3am. When he had looked at his alarm clock he'd misread it. He had to sit in his front room for an hour waiting to be picked up. On arrival at work he was in good spirits until he was told he had in fact booked the day off as annual leave. So the Boss took him straight back home again.

MAD WORLD 12
GARY WANTS A COMPANY BIKE

I have just written this answer to my nephew, Gary, who is keen on one of the bikes we use at work for his Sunday paper round.

Dear Gary,
Your Dad said you wanted to know what happens to old company bicycles. I have made some inquiries this week and have the following information for you.

Old company bicycles used to be sold to any employees who wished to buy them.

Then the company got jumpy about being sued if someone had an accident on one of our ex-company bicycles so the practice of selling them was stopped. Quite why the bicycles should be considered unsafe in civilian hands when they had been considered safe whilst being used for deliveries is beyond me. I can only assume that there was a risk that the bicycles might get used by someone who had not had the advanced bicycle training deemed necessary for handling such beasts of the highway.

The next idea was to send the old bicycles to third world countries where apparently it didn't matter if a few of the inhabitants had accidents when using our old equipment.

The last idea we heard about was when the new Hot Rod 3 speeders were put into use. All the old single speed bicycles were cut up into little bits and thrown away. The 3 speeders are logged and so getting you one of those is pretty much out of the question. The old single speed bikes were, eventually, what we call 'shagged.'

However, I am able to offer you the once in a lifetime opportunity to buy a single speeder, complete with sandwich basket on the front. You can a,) have all the parts free of charge and build it yourself, but you must paint it a different colour. It is red at the moment. Or maybe rusty red, I'm not sure as I haven't seen it. Or option b,) is the same beast of a machine, fully assembled and ready for many years of happy Sunday paper delivering for the hard negotiated price of £40. I have no doubt you could one day make a profit on this if you keep it long enough. They don't tend to come up on the Antiques Road Show just yet.

I'm sorry you must have it in a different colour than red but, we have all the red ones.

I am also sorry to only be able to offer a single speeder but again, that is out of my hands. These are the rules of the highway. And you may be so pleased with your bicycle that you may ride it during the week as well. Bicycle mounted paperboys are allowed to overtake pedestrians, horses and milk floats but, definitely not Hot Rod 3 speeder mounted colleagues of mine. I am also not able to provide panniers as I think someone would notice in the morning.

I have an alternative suggestion for you. Some bicycles these days have trailers, so perhaps you could get one of those. They seem like a good, modern idea.

If you take the fully built bicycle option it would have to be cash, sterling, as we cannot take credit cards and we don't do terms.

Hope this is some use as I have left no mail bag unturned to get you a deal.

Look forward to hearing from you,
Regards,
Steve.
PS: Glad you didn't ask me to get you a van.

In true Rolls-Royce fashion there is no number 13.

MAD WORLD 12a
TAKING MUM SHOPPING

It is my job to take Mum shopping every 3 or 4 weeks due, I expect, to the fact that I must be the only one in the family with a car. Coming from a family of 6 boys, we were always brought up to treat each other as fairly as possible and that is a fantasy that still exists to this day. I take Mum to Sainsbury's to buy the coffee and then my brothers go round to drink it. Maybe that's why I don't like coffee, it leaves a nasty taste.

I usually drop Mum at the door at Sainsbury's. Then I either go off and do something else for an hour, or just park up as far away as possible in the carpark to avoid all the Mums in a hurry and so that my car doesn't get scratched. I then sit and read. Mum doesn't need me to push the trolley so I like her to wander around at her own pace. But I do go in to help her through the checkout by unloading the trolley and re-loading it on the other side. I like to put all the goods on the conveyer belt in some sort of order, the order in which I wish to receive them at the other end.

This week, Mum got around in record time and, when I found her, she was already at the checkout. She had her head down in the trolley, arms flailing like mad piling the stuff on to the conveyer belt. She looked like a human dynamo but without the brain switched on. The conveyer belt resembled a jumble sale. It reminded me of the time I took her to the supermarket and we put so much on to the conveyer belt that it stopped and we were politely asked to take some of the items off.

Unable to do anything about this end of the operation, I took the trolley which was now empty, through to the other side ready to start filling it again. As I passed through, the cashier asked if I needed any help packing. I said that I should be OK as I usually manage quite well. She hit the starter pedal and we were off. All the stuff I didn't want came first. Bread in one bag and into the trolley. Biscuits and sweets [for the grandchildren's visits I expect] into another bag and into the trolley. Now for the heavier stuff. After doing another bag full, I didn't want to put it on top of the bread or biscuits so, starting to panic, I pulled the child seat down and plonked this bag on to that. Must have plonked too hard. Without any warning a yoghurt pot suddenly took off. The most enormous yoghurt pot you ever did see. And it was going at a velocity NASA would have been proud of. I wished it could have been a soup tin but it had to be a yoghurt pot. I saw it take off and I heard it land smack on the floor. I looked down and could see it had a nice split across part of the lid and down one side. The contents were making a bid for freedom with a gloop, gloop, gloop, out onto the floor. I have never had an experience like this and didn't know what to do next. Besides, I still had other groceries coming at me at an alarming rate. Mum would know what to do, she had had years of going shopping before I started coming along to help.

"Mum." I called. She didn't hear me. I looked up and she looked busy? The cashier was scanning and I was packing and Mum looked busy? But she had nothing to do. And the cashier was scanning an awful lot faster than I was packing.

"Mum." I called a second time. This time she heard me.
"What is it?" she replied.
"One of your enormous tubs of yoghurt has hit the deck." I said.

Thinking she may not cotton on to the implications of that statement I added: "And split."

"Never mind," she said, "I like a bit of yoghurt on my cereal in the mornings."

Magic. I hope I'm that switched off if I get to her age.

MAD WORLD 14

ICE CREAM FOR SALE

Follow up from previous M/W: Gary has decided to go for the fully built £40 bike for his paper round so my colleague will have to get busy. The mechanic did not get the job at Goudhurst. I wonder if his chances would have been better if he had taken his certificates along.

You may not know this but all the Balls Ice Cream vans live in a shed along Bulverhythe Road in St. Leonards and set off to find their sites across the UK every morning before most people are out of bed. One Sunday morning, the 12th of March, I was on my way to get the Bentley out for a trip to the old racing circuit/museum at Brooklands in Weybridge. It looked like the gritting lorry had been out all night as possible sleet showers had been forecast for the day, following on from an overnight frost. I had the heater on in the Volvo, the heated seat was switched on and the outside temperature gauge was showing zero with the little orange frost warning light on. I was wearing a jumper, coat, woolly hat and gloves. I counted 5 Balls Ice Cream vans setting off along Bexhill road.

If that wasn't mad I don't know what is. As we crossed the Ashdown Forest on our way to Brooklands we saw a solitary Balls Ice Cream van in a car park. I looked at the driver as we passed by. What a long way to go to read your Sunday paper.

MAD WORLD 15
TELEPHONE KEEPS RINGING

When we moved to our bungalow we thought what a fantastic idea it would be to go ex-directory with our phone number. At least then we would only get phone calls from people we wanted to hear from.

Do you know why companies do competitions where you write your name, address and telephone number on to a postcard and post it?

I could tell you.

MAD WORLD 16
SUNDAY NEWSPAPERS

The local newspaper seller in the village that I work in operates from a shed in the village. He and his son deliver the papers to a lot of their customers. Other customers collect their papers from the shed. The papers left in the shed for collection are marked with customers' names and there are, sometimes, a spare paper or two to sell to someone passing by. In the past, I have sold papers to people visiting the village. Having been on holiday from work for the past week, I haven't heard from any of the villagers but they know where I am if they need me. At 10am on Sunday our phone rang:

Friendly Female Customer/ Friend of mine from the village: "Steve, I've got a problem. I know how good you are at sorting problems out for people and......."

Me: "Just get on with it, what's your problem?" [I was, after all, about to go outside and wash both of our Volvo cars].

FFC: "Sorry, I was just trying to butter you up a bit first. When I went down for my paper this morning it didn't have the 'sport' in it. [I guess that is the Sunday supplement] So I took one out of another paper."

She went on to tell me the name that was written on the other paper which was, unfortunately, collected while she was still there. She described the people who collected it and the vehicle they were traveling in. The people collecting the paper were not the people whose name was on the paper.

FFC: "When I got home I found my sports supplement inside my paper after all so now I ought to get the spare sports pages to the other people. Do you know who the people were who collected the paper?"

Me: "No I don't. They don't sound like any of the neighbours of the people whose paper it was."

FFC: "I have phoned the people whose name was on the paper but got no reply. I thought if I could get hold of the people who collected it I could tell them what I've done. Do you think people worry if they don't get their sports pages?"

Me: "Well, you did."

FFC: "What do you think I should do?"

Me: "You take the spare magazine back and put it in the shed."

FFC: "I thought if I do take it back, I will take it tomorrow as I don't want to see Graham. He will go mad if he knows what I have done."

Me: "You should take it back now."

FFC: "But I'll bump into Graham and he'll do his nut. I'll leave it until tomorrow."

Me: "You take it back now so that if the other people ring Graham to say they didn't get their magazine, he can say he has one in the shed. If you see anyone when you get there you just say that you got home and found 2 magazines in your paper and thought it would be best to return it straight away in case someone is missing theirs. That way no one in the village will know what you've been up to and you don't have to spend the rest of the day worrying about it."

I received another phone call later that morning to say she had followed my advice and how Graham had told her she needn't have bothered. So after doing something definitely not right, she came out of it looking quite good.

I never knew Sunday papers could cause so much trouble.

MAD WORLD 17
POORLY CHICKEN

A female colleague who worked at our office for a short while had a pet chicken. One morning, it was clear that this particular colleague wasn't her usual self. She was obviously quite anxious and upset. I asked her what was wrong. Apparently it was her chicken. She had taken her chicken to the vet because it had hurt its leg. The vet had kept it in, so as to give it some treatment, keep it under observation and, no doubt, provide her with a huge bill. To try and help, as usual, I tried to give an alternative view of the situation. I told the young lady that she needn't have wasted time and money taking her chicken to the vet, as I felt sure that we could have sorted its dodgy leg out for her. Either before it went in the oven or after it came out. She didn't speak to me much after that.

MAD WORLD 18
WHATS A NUMBER 2?

I had a thought today about why it takes me so long to do my round in the way I do it. I think it's because I deliver to people, not just letterboxes.

At the risk of Mad World becoming a daily update, I will give you today's enormous embarrassment. I do sometimes wonder what it would be like to just go quietly through life un-noticed.

I walked into a property today, as I usually do, and went to hand the mail to the very attractive girl/ young lady sitting at the table.

"Steve, I had a dream about you last night." she said.

"You most certainly shouldn't be calling it a dream if I was in it." I replied.

The very attractive young lady continued with: "I dreamt you had a number 2."

I stood there stunned. 'What was a lovely girl like this doing dreaming of me on the toilet?' I thought. Seeing my obvious distress, she went on to explain to the very dim postman that a number 2 is a haircut. Good Lord. Maybe if I'd had children, it would have kept me more up to date. I haven't been in a Barber's shop for over 30 years. I always thought I would come out looking like a Charlie.

I think I was right.

MAD WORLD 19
LET ME OUT

It's my job to drop bags of mail off for 2 town walks. Both drop off points are on the wrong side of the road for me, the right hand side. This means I have to cross both lines of traffic when pulling back out to continue on my way. I have to wait for a suitable gap in the traffic or, if I'm running really late and the traffic is heavy, I just have to hope some kind soul will let me out.

This morning, I was waiting to pull out of the driveway of the second drop off point and the traffic was nose to tail in both directions. It was a damp, gloomy morning and I was already late. I spotted a customer of mine coming towards me in the traffic on my side of the road. 'What luck,' I thought, 'he's bound to let me out.' I watched and waited. He started waving his hand so I knew he had seen me. He kept waving and looked at me through the passenger side window as he passed by the end of my bonnet. I raised a hesitant hand in a mixture of acknowledgement and disbelief.

Having been brought up to try and see the other chap's point of view in life I will have a go.

Happy Town Resident sets off in his big, comfy car to go to work at his nice warm, dry little indoor job. 'Oh look,' he thinks to himself, 'there's Steve trying to get out of that driveway. He'll be there all day with this traffic. I'll give him a wave to show him I have seen him. He appears to be looking my way but I don't think he has seen me yet as he hasn't waved back. I'll try to catch his eye as I go past and...... Oh good, he just spotted me at the last moment as I think I saw him raise his hand. That'll have cheered him up.'

MAD WORLD 20
FULL SIZE BRIDESMAIDS

I sometimes do weddings and odd jobs for people who know I've got the Rolls and the Bentley. I had an occasion this year that really had me chuckling, but luckily, that was after I'd put the 'phone' down.

I'm usually contacted a few months before a job and I ask questions like 'When is it? Where is it? How many trips to the church? How many Bridesmaids? And where is the reception?' At this stage there may be one or two bridesmaids but bridesmaids are funny things and tend to multiply faster than bunny rabbits. When the final details are discussed, I often find myself being asked to squeeze too many in. And how about the Mother of the Bride? Can she come too? It gets to the point where you could have one in the front, three in the back, two in the boot and the biggest one strapped to the roof. Later this year, I'm even expected to squeeze in the Mother of the Groom as well. I'm currently back tracking on that one. Fast.

Now, whilst I will agree that young ladies and squeezing can be most delightful when put together, you can take it from me that bridesmaids and squeezing is most definitely not to be recommended. Bridesmaids like to look just so when they are all posh frock and lipstick. They don't give two hoots about what they get up to or look like afterwards, but they're jolly fussy creatures beforehand. If you try to squeeze too many in to the car, their dresses get creased and they aren't happy when they toddle up the aisle. Another thing that's guaranteed to happen is what a bridesmaid does when they are in the front with me. They will always pull down the sun visor to check their lipstick in the vanity mirror. All the spare ribbon, that I have carefully rolled up and tucked behind the sun visor, lands in their lap.

The last wedding I did was to be in the Bentley which can't accommodate as many people in comfort as the Rolls. I made contact with the Father of the Bride a week before kick-off.

"How many Bridesmaids will there be?" I enquired.

"More than we originally expected." he replied.

You don't say. I needed to know how big they were, or what I mean is, how wide, as that determines how many will fit on the back seat.

"How big are they?" I enquired.

"There are 3 full size, one much smaller and a child." he replied.

I went on to explain that we would need to reduce the number because nowadays, with all the legal and insurance rules and regulations, it isn't good practice to travel in a car fitted with seatbelts with a child sitting on someone's knee. We sorted it all out amicably and arranged for the child to travel in another vehicle with the Mother of the Bride. When I came off the phone, my imagination kicked off. What does a full size bridesmaid look like? Would I know one if I saw one? Which bit is full size? All of it or part of it? Which part? I have had one or two over the years that could have been described as full size at the front and it can be the highlight of the day to adjust the rear view mirror accordingly, beware that wedding car.........he may not be looking where he's going. I imagined some Benny Hill music playing as I chased the 3 full size bridesmaids around the car. I imagined spending many happy minutes pushing their full size posteriors through the back door of the Bentley. What a great shame none of this came to fruition on the day.

MAD WORLD 21
RING THE BELL. WHAT BELL?

Just a bit of fun but I thought you might like to hear it.

There's a property in the town which is on the first part of my delivery with some new people who moved in towards the end of last year. I got on very well with the previous occupants but this new lot suffered from short arms and deep pockets at Christmas, which was a great shame. Let's hope for better things next Christmas. However, they have managed to scrape enough together to have a bit of an extension put on the front of the house, yippee. This meant I had several weeks of fiddling about with a little plastic box with a lid into which I had to try and squeeze their mail. Thankfully, once the extension was completed I was able to start using the letter box on the front door again.

They had a packet one morning so I had to ring the bell. What bell?

Bang, Bang, Bang, I had to thump on the door. And again and again. Eventually, I got a reply.

Customer: "Hello mate."

Me: "If you were wondering what the builder left off, it was the bell."

Customer: "Got one coming tomorrow."

Several days later, here we go again. Bang, Bang, Bang.

Customer: "Hello mate."

Me: "I was forgetting, tomorrow never comes does it?"

This morning, Bang, Bang, Bang.

Customer: "Do you know the bell's coming?"

Me: "No, I don't, you hum it and I'll see if I recognise it."

MAD WORLD 22
SHEIK THE BOTTLE

I have a property on my round which is owned by a couple who I don't see often enough to be able to recognise them in the street. They have lived and worked abroad for all the time I have been delivering in the village. They are about to return home in the next 3-4 weeks as I believe he must be retiring from his job. I am not hot on geography but they have told me they have been based in Aboo Derby which I always thought was in the Midlands but they say it is jolly hot there so it can't be. The best bit is, they wish to bring me home a present for all the good service I've given them with their post. Yes, really. Now do you see why it takes me so long to get around on my round? It must be some kind of record for me to get a present for all the good service I've given when the people were never even in the country.

"Do I drink, smoke or gamble?" I was asked. Is that it then? Is that what really makes the world go round? No wonder I find life such a struggle at times. I explained that, unfortunately, I am a rather sad bunny and don't enjoy any of those vices.

"How about something to wear?" they enquired.

"Like what?" I asked.

"How about one of those robes the chaps wear out there?" They suggested.

Hell's Bells, they're looking to dress me up like Sheik the Bottle.

I know I have several motorbikes but I'm clean out of camels at the moment.

"Well, I really don't know when I would wear it." I said.

"How about wearing it to bed?" They suggested.
"Well I do think that could prove to be a bit of a passion killer if I arrive in the bedroom dressed in one of those." I replied.

Lord knows what I'll end up with. There's hope though as on hearing this tale, a good friend suggested I ask for a Belly Dancer. Boy oh boy, I've certainly got the belly for her to dance on. I am frantically trying to contact Aboo Derby to put forward this excellent suggestion.

First a few updates.

Now that I send all these Mad Worlds out with no addresses showing, we don't know who we all are. It's OK for me because I have a list on the back of an envelope, but if I lose the list then I'll be in the same boat as you. How will we know who we all are? How will we recognise each other? Maybe you could all grow ginger beards? Mine saves me a hell of a lot of bother in the mornings. I believe the Masons go on about being square and in a square and being in the same square as someone else. I've checked in the mirror and there was nothing very square to be seen there.

I did have another idea but had to abandon that as well. Put it this way, we can't all go around winking at each other because half the chaps I work with wink at me in the mornings and it gives me the creeps. Yes, I work with a bunch of winkers. And you villagers can't go around winking. Imagine sitting down at the Harvest Supper in October and winking to the chap opposite. If he doesn't give you a slap, his wife certainly will. More thought required, I think.

My nephew, Gary, backed out of the deal for a company bike. Shame. I had to go to my supplier and give him the bad news. We always allow a fourteen-day cooling-off period, but Gary missed the deadline and was in danger of losing his deposit if he had paid one. I think Gary was put off by the single speed when he would have preferred a 3 speed. My supplier has a spare 3 speed frame but no wheels. Isn't that typical? So often in life we find ourselves with a vital bit missing. Or, as in this case, 2 vital bits. Bit like Oliver our cat, poor chap. Chop, Chop, Ollie.

I saw the customer today who hadn't let me out into the traffic last week. I told him that next time, instead of waving his hand up and down, he should wave it from side to side and let me out in front of him. Hope that sank in.

MAD WORLD 23
SOME PEOPLE JOG. THEY NEED TO

I was thinking today, as I delivered to the big Christian Centre on my round, about a girl I saw there a while back who was out for a jog. Those who can't run, jog instead. And they tend to be the ones that need to. She was jogging along the tarmac road that goes around the outside of all the buildings. I would guess she was aiming on doing a circuit. As I came up behind her I could see how grateful she must have been for the enormous amount of elastic that goes into tracksuit bottoms. I, however, was imagining the enormous number of pies she must have eaten to get her track suit bottoms to look like they did. And those pies didn't look half as appetising now from where I was sitting. As I drew alongside I could see she was a funny colour and, as the window of the van was down, I asked "Are you alright?"

"I'm trying to lose some weight." She replied.
"Best go round again then." I suggested.

MAD WORLD 24
DIY AND CHEAP LUNCH

Here in the South East, we're facing a drought this summer. No rain has fallen for about 3 years, so they say. The water board wants us all on water meters, we could be looking at stand pipes in the street and I will be shot if I wash the Rolls.

So how come the Grass Track Racing this weekend has been cancelled due to a waterlogged field and the local Caravan Park is only half open because they are only able to use hardstanding pitches as the grass pitches are too wet?

I saw a friend of mine getting bits and bobs for the job he had to do today. He was purchasing various items from the timber yard including a fence post. My friend is, according to his invoices, a professional at gardening services, putting up fences and also sheds. Patios can also be dealt with. I think he would consider himself to be an expert. Unfortunately, my friend in Brighton has explained the word 'expert' to me: X is the unknown quantity, and a spurt is a drip under pressure.

Half an hour later, I was delivering down a lane when I saw this particular drip coming towards me in his car and still towing his posh Ifor Williams trailer. I stood in the lane as he drew up. He was looking a bit embarrassed. I looked in the trailer and spotted the fence post. My friend was looking even more embarrassed. I only spoke 3 words and he said nothing but nodded his head as he pulled away. "Wrong size post?"

It reminded me of the time I made a Charlie of myself at B&Q. I was attempting a bit of 'damage it yourself 'in my garage. I measured up the exact length of shelving I required and went off to B&Q. I purchased the exact length of shelf I required and took it back to my car. My car was not, unfortunately, the exact length I now needed it to be. I had to queue at the refund desk with this enormous shelf stood beside me and politely ask if I could change it for a much shorter one. One that I could actually take home.

Another incident we had at B&Q was the time we thought we'd take our 5 litre can of wood preserver to the car in one of the shop's trollies. The trolley wouldn't go up the lowered kerb. The trouble was, we only found this out at speed. The 5 litre can took off, launching itself away from the trolley, hit the deck and split the lid. We looked at the stain for years afterwards whenever we visited the retail park.

Yesterday, one of my horsey customers was all done up for a trip out in the car. She did look good.

"Where are we off to today?" I enquired.

The lady went on to tell me: "Yes Steve, it was a toss-up between going out with you or my husband but I'm afraid this time you lost out because he was free." I hadn't realised I was considered expensive.

"Never mind." I replied.

She carried on: "Four of us are going for a pub lunch. It's a deal that's being run by the newspaper we get. We can get a 2 course dinner for £5 at a selection of pubs."

"Hope you enjoy it." I replied. Never mind the petrol to get there and back in their limousine.

Today, she was back in her riding gear and coming up the lane on Red Rum.

"How was your dinner for a fiver?" I shouted.

"Very nice but the portions were very small." she replied.

Only one answer to that:
"What do you expect for a fiver?" I asked.

The next bit made my day. How the posh people live. She finished up with:
"I was still hungry when I got home so I had to have some scrambled eggs."

MAD WORLD 25
SPECIAL APRIL FOOLS' DAY EDITION

Being a very keen motorcyclist and having played a very active part in a number of accidents over the years, I have always considered the most important item of protective gear to be my crash helmet. Rather like the most important part of a motorcycle being the nut that holds the handlebars. Riding without a crash helmet 40 years ago may have been OK but it definitely isn't in modern day traffic. Today a colleague started spouting off with:

"I only wear a crash helmet when I ride my motorcycle because Mr. Policeman says I have to."

I hit straight back with:

"That's because, if you have an accident with your motorcycle and hit your head on the ground, you might start talking nonsense."

At work, we have a rest room and kitchen upstairs where people can go, if they have time, to have something to eat or drink. There is never any need for people to sit at their sorting frame and eat. It would be odd for someone to do so and is something I've hardly ever seen in my 18 years on the job. This morning, being April Fools' Day, one old chap thought it would be a laugh to sit at his frame and have breakfast and make out he was confusing April Fools' Day with Shrove Tuesday. As he sat and ate his pancakes, a colleague asked him what was occurring.

"It's April Fools' Day," he replied, "it's traditional to eat pancakes on April Fools' Day."

Now I know I'm not the sharpest at times but I thought the idea of April Fools' Day was to make a fool out of someone else.....not yourself. I'm not sure if they should be in the asylum or I should be. But one thing's for sure, I'm seriously considering writing fiction instead of writing about real life as that might not sound so ridiculous.

MAD WORLD 26
IT'S A PLUNGER

I had a long period last summer of working 6 day weeks so only had Sunday off. Monday to Saturday means getting up at 3.30am and leaving at 4 am. Of course, in reality, I get up at 3.40 am and leave at 4.10 am, in a hurry. Sunday, therefore, should mean a much more relaxing start to the day. We had about 3 Sundays over one 6 week period when we got up in the morning and found the kitchen sink blocked. I was told by Jayne: "leave it to me." I then watched as the sink had kettle after kettle of boiling water emptied into it. This was then followed by the sink, which was full to the brim, being emptied by having the water ladled out and into a bucket. Trying to eat your Rice Krispies or porridge while all this is taking place is not the relaxing start to the day I had been hoping for. Time to get a plunger.

There is a very handy little shop that sells this type of thing in the town where I work. I went in on the way home one day to buy one. The man said: "I don't have any toilet plungers at the moment, only sink plungers. And I only appear to have the expensive ones of those left." I guess he must have had a bit of a rush on plungers. Well, I didn't know there was such a thing as a toilet plunger. 'Whatever size must they be?' I wondered. They must be enormous to fit over the toilet seat. I feel sure I would have to stand on top of a step ladder to operate one. Anyway, the man plonked a sink plunger onto the counter and I gave him my £5 note and awaited my 50 pence change. The plunger was standing up as he turned towards the till. I looked at the plunger. I had never had a plunger before and couldn't resist playing with it. I pushed down on it. Then I tried to pull it back up. It was stuck. It just wouldn't budge. I had paid my £4.50 and now it was stuck to the counter. Oh dear.

The man turned to give me my change and looked at the plunger and then looked at me. I gave him a smile. I could tell what he was thinking. It was plastered across his forehead in great big letters: 'Oh no, we've got one of them in today have we?' He pulled on the plunger. It didn't move. We both pulled on it and it still didn't move. Must be a good one then, I thought. If only I could take it home. We finally got it to shift a bit with both of us pushing it. We had to push it bit by bit across the counter to the edge where, thankfully, it popped off. There aren't many shops I dare go into near where I work these days.

MAD WORLD 27
BLOCKED EARS

Have you ever wondered why you can never get an appointment at the Doctor's? Try this for size:

I rang the surgery this week and, not wanting to take a Doctor's appointment up, asked if I could have an appointment with the Nurse to get my ear syringed. I explained that I have, as before, been putting the drops in and all that had done was turn the wax to glue. Here we are in the middle of April and the next available appointment with the Nurse is mid-May. As I need good hearing for the 27th of April, I said that I felt that was a long time to wait. The receptionist told me I could have an appointment with a Doctor the week after next so I went for that instead. Two hours later the phone rang:

Receptionist: "Sorry but I shouldn't have booked you in to have your ear syringed."

Me: "Why not?"

Receptionist: "According to the new guidelines and procedures, I should only book you in to see a Doctor, then he'll look in your ear and tell you if it needs to be syringed."

I was speechless.

Receptionist: "So I've cancelled the appointment you made earlier and you can come next week to see the Doctor. If he says your ear needs to be syringed then, you can have an appointment to have it done on another day."

I have 2 ears so I wonder if he looks in both ears on the same day or whether that will mean another appointment? I think, with things as they are, I had better keep quiet about my piles.

MAD WORLD 28
NOW I CAN HEAR AGAIN

I very nearly didn't do this one because you had to be there to believe it. So this is just for my records to make sure that I remember it in future. I went to the Doctor today and asked him to look in my ear. Since the water shortage and the hose pipe ban, Doctors are no longer allowed to syringe ears. So much for doing my bit with a Hippo airbag in the cistern to save using so much water when flushing the loo. And one bath a month. Now they aren't allowed to do my ears.

We now have to go to the Hospital to have the wax sucked out or the chap puts on a miner's lamp to see down the ear canal and then scrapes it out. I explained that I have to have good hearing for the track day with the Bentley next week or I will have to cancel.

After much consultation with the other Doctor, long enough, in fact, to have done the ear, they said: "Pop back on Monday, and if you put some drops in the other ear we'll do that as well." Beware........Make sure the Doctor you get is a petrol head.

MAD WORLD 29
EVERYBODY NEEDS A KETTLE

So good to be able to finish the week with some good news.

It has been a constant worry in our house as we've watched the decline of the Post Office Counters. The main crown offices have been disappearing from high streets all over the country and the sub-post offices have been doing the same in rural areas. Post Office Counters have had a hard time. They got a rough deal over paying out pensions as more and more people have the money paid into bank accounts. Stamps can be bought when you buy your paper or your petrol and the next thing will be that they'll lose the opportunity to issue television licences as well. What can be done to plug the revenue gap? Much has been tried in recent months, including selling you insurance for your car if you drive, or a home phone if you don't, so you can phone someone for a lift. Success, however, has come from a very unlikely source.

Our local Post Office has had an unexpected runaway success this past week as, in less than a week, they have sold out of ......kettles.

Well it struck me as barmy anyway.

Two for tea and tea for two,

Tea for me and tea for you.

MAD WORLD 30
FIVE BELLIES

First of all, one of the replies I had this week about the news I sent everyone regarding the publisher had a brilliant 2 sentences which I would like to share with you. I've never met the lady as she's a friend of a friend.

She wrote: Put me down for a signed first edition of Oliver's Tail. What's it about?

Ok, I know I shouldn't write these after a bad day at the office but just consider it as therapy for me.

Here we are in the middle of May and today the delivery was more like a Christmas delivery. I didn't get back to the office until almost 2 o'clock. I know we should all be happy bunnies because we have had our annual pay rise, but that was against the wishes of our union. It wasn't agreed to as it wasn't considered to be enough. But our caring, sharing employer paid us what they wanted. Now, no doubt, when the union ballots us for strike action, we will get even more bad press. One wag in the office spent the past 2 weeks trying to convince everyone that we were going to get an £80 a week pay rise. I suggested that if that were the case then it must mean either a] it would be £80 between us or b] someone had put the decimal point in the wrong place. It was of course, nearer to b]. And that is before Mr. Blair takes his share to help fund his next election campaign.

In an organisation such as ours, it is normal practice, when things are going against us, to blame the Boss. This we do, on average, about once every 10 minutes.

We've had various affectionate names for our Boss over the years such as:

The Fat Controller because he is supposed to control the smooth running of the office.

Lord Lucan because no one knows where he is.

Mr. Punch, because he is a bit of a cartoon character who has a habit of turning nasty and bashing us when we least deserve it.

And the old favourite, Five Bellies, because of the size of shirt he has to wear. On a morning like today when I ride a motorbike to work, I follow my mate, the PHG, through the office as he unlocks all the doors up to the locker room where I change for work. At 4.30 am, as we climb the stairs, we chat happily about the joyous day ahead. This morning, the PHG told me he was on his own again today as Five Bellies had got the day off. And we had a delivery to cover. PHG also told me that, as we were going to be short staffed today, he had asked Five Bellies why he couldn't work on Friday and have Saturday off instead. Five Bellies had then told PHG:

"I can't have Saturday as my day off as I only come in for 2 hours on a Saturday."

Where can I sign up for a job like that?

Five Bellies recently changed his daily driver [Vehicle he drives to work in. A trip that's all of 1/2 a mile]. He tends to favour the big 4 wheel drive vehicles which have more robust suspension to support his rather generous frame. Rumour has it in the office that he eats all the pies because he's the only one who can afford to buy them.

Anyway, Five Bellies went into to our local Post Office a couple of Saturdays ago to tax his new vehicle. He went to my Jayne's counter. He puffed out his chest and said to Jayne:

"You don't know who I am do you?"

Jayne gave him one of her looks.

He went on with: "I'm Steve's boss."

Jayne replied with: "What are you doing in here at this time on a Saturday then? I bet my Steve is still out delivering".

Personally, I won't have a bad word said about him and I think he is a jolly fine chap. And how pleased I am to be doing his brother's wedding later this year with both cars. Five Bellies is paying. So I'll help myself to a healthy slice of the big bonus he gets for keeping our overtime down to a minimum.

I'm feeling better already.

MAD WORLD 31
THE WORLD CUP

Here we go again with another World Cup. Yippee. Time to get all patriotic. That'll make a change from idiotic.

I know all about being patriotic. There is a chap living in Ninfield who does Patriotic very well. He has posters all over the entrance to his drive. Vote UKIP they say, keep the United Kingdom independent. Save the Pound, we don't want the Euro. He even has stickers all over his car with the same UKIP and Save the Pound messages. This, unfortunately, is where he loses his credibility. He drives a little French Citroen car. I remember watching the local UKIP candidate during the last election, trying to hand out leaflets in our local high street and wondering why there weren't many takers. He had posters all over his French Peugeot car.

Now, with the World Cup Football Tournament rapidly approaching, I have already seen the signs that the must have accessory for your car is a stick on flag. Your car really won't reach the end of the street unless you have a flag or two.

We had a day out yesterday in the Rolls and attended the largest gathering this end of the country for Rolls-Royce and Bentley motorcars. Over 300 cars. I didn't hear the word 'football' mentioned all day. Not a single flag in sight. Back at work today, I was thinking how I could have approached the day in the manner that most of my football loving work colleagues would have done.

Three hundred Rolls and Bentley motorcars parked up and along come Steve and Jayne in their 1957 Silver Cloud, complete with a flag stuck to each window. Steve & Jayne written in big lettering across the windscreen. The windows are down with the radio blaring as loud as possible. Out jumps Steve in his sunglasses, shorts, shirt hanging out and ankle socks, out jumps Jayne chewing gum. You know it might work if only I could get something other than *The Archers* on my 50 year old valve radio.

MAD WORLD 32
SHORT OF WATER AND CATCH THE VILLAINS

Despite getting wet through on several days last week whilst out on delivery, the water shortage continues. There is something quite special about working outside all morning in a force 9 gale, lashed by horizontal rain, wet through to the underpants, water running into the holes at the top of the body and out of the holes lower down. Then, when you get home you put the television on and the weather man says "Sorry, but that lot we had this morning has done no good, wrong sort of rain." This is followed by the man from the water board giving us a few more tips on how to not do things with water. Don't clean your teeth, have a bath or wash the car. I'm doing OK with 2 out of 3 of those. How about you? Answers on a postcard might be best as you wouldn't want to come too close right now. His next suggestion had me really foxed. Only put as much water in your kettle as you need. What does he think I've been doing with the bit that's left over?

Moving on, do you remember the saga of our local Post Office selling out of kettles?
Well, the following week they sold out of DVD players and were down to the last toaster. So they phoned an emergency order through to the supplier. They were then told that they had been sent the electrical items by mistake and should not have displayed them. Our local office pointed out that there was better profit in kettles than padded envelopes and in fact, they were now meeting their targets at long last with regard to turnover and profit.

Please, please, could they have some more kettles? The case was won and a further delivery was dispatched with one condition. A man was sent to sort out the display. The electrical items were moved to a less obvious corner of the office where, hopefully, they wouldn't sell so quickly. With all this madness going on it is no wonder that, on more than one occasion, little old ladies have arrived at the counter and asked, "Excuse me, do you sell stamps?"

I suggested that so as to further improve the turnover and profit figures, the answer to the little old ladies' question should be, "Yes, but only these limited edition packs of 12."

Much excitement in the Town last week with the arrival of real cops and robbers. I had great difficulty returning to the office at lunch time with the High Street closed off as a crime scene. A colleague informed me that there had been a shootout in the High Street when armed Police stopped 3 robbers from robbing the Nationwide Building Society. It was like Beirut I was told. Wow! I didn't know there was a Nationwide in Beirut. My colleague went on to say that the Police had followed the robbers all the way down from London after a tip off. I puzzled on the way home as to how it would stand up in court. How can you prosecute robbers who hadn't in fact committed a robbery? I also wondered why armed Police wear baseball caps. The evening news told us a bit more about the events but it was the local paper I bought the following day that gave us the real story. It related how the Metropolitan Police had cornered these 3 robbers and arrested them and then removed bundles of money from their car.

Now, this is only my opinion, but as I see it, the robbers must have been local chaps who had nicked the money in London and thought they would pay it into the local Nationwide Building Society and get a bit of interest over the bank holiday weekend. Time will tell if I'm right.

Bit of excitement last Saturday. Caught a chap out on my round who was completely stark bollock naked in his kitchen. Unfortunately, I only get really interested when I catch a chap stark bollock naked in somebody else's kitchen.

MAD WORLD 33
FORGET THE PENSION. CONCENTRATE ON THE WORLD CUP

I hate going back to work after a bank holiday so, in case you feel the same, this is for you. Oh dear, it looks like Steve is enjoying his work again.

Yesterday, we employees all received a letter from our pensions department telling us not to worry about what we read in the press and not to worry about our pensions. Oh good, all under control then. Today, we were all called to an emergency meeting.

We were told that due to the anticipated increase in mechanisation over the coming months and years, we should now be worried about our jobs. What a considerate place to work. They only want us to worry about one thing at a time.

Flags on cars. Remember them?

Looking on the positive side, as I always do, judging by how many weeks the flags have been on some cars, I can only assume that the World Cup Competition must be due to finish any day now. I have had a bit of correspondence on this flag issue. One good friend emailed to say that he understood what one flag was a sign of, and also what two flags indicated, but he had seen a chap driving a vehicle with three flags and didn't know what to make of it. Again, as an employee of this wonderful company I work for, I can only come up with one answer to the question. The chap driving a vehicle with 3 flags sounds like management material to me.

Rumour has it that one of the big cheeses at the top of our company came to us from the Football Association [F.A.]. What a pity that, since joining our organisation, he seems to have trained the managers to do sweet F.A.

Our manager once had a couple of weeks off with a bad neck. One wag in the office suggested that he must have pulled a muscle whilst having a doze in his office.

Now, where's that employee opinion survey I have to fill in and return by Friday?

P.S. Latest Neighbourhood Watch email says 2 out of 3 of the robbers from last week are local men. The other chap was of no fixed abode but previously lived in London. How far out was I on that?

MAD WORLD 34
SCORING IS DIFFICULT

Look out, it's the World Cup subject again. At least I can think of 2 positives.

1, When, England qualify for the final, we can look forward to the quietest roads we've had for decades whilst the game is being played.

2, When England lose the final, all those patriotic English fans will experience the same disappointment and distress that I experienced when all the patriotic English sat by and watched Rolls-Royce and Bentley get sold to the Germans. +

Talking of disappointment.

Years ago, when I was returning to the office one day on foot after doing a town delivery, I happened upon a customer I knew who was emerging from the *Friday-Ad* shop with his five year old son. Down our way, the *Friday-Ad* is a free to pick up advertiser which contains all manner of things to buy privately. The *Friday-Ad* shop contains all types of stationary and often toys for the youngsters.

The Father said: "We've just been in to look at the Lego."

I enquired "Did you buy any?"

"No," the Father replied, "That was the purpose of the visit, I wanted to take him in to look and then come out without buying any as I just wanted to get him used to the disappointments in life."

I digress. Back to the World Cup.

Either my lack of knowledge of football is worse than we thought or some unkind soul has been pulling someone's leg.

One day last week when I was having a particularly bad day, I went for about an hour whilst out on delivery without checking in the back of the van to see what packets I had. Unfortunately, this resulted in my having to re-visit about 4 calls on the way back to the office. One such call was to an elderly lady who is disabled now and wheelchair bound. As she isn't usually up when I deliver, we have to have a little chat if I ever call back on her.

"I've been watching my team [the Swiss] in the Football World Cup," she said, "but they seem to be having trouble getting the ball into the goal."

'Bet they aren't the only team having that problem,' I thought to myself.

She continued: "I'm sure that in previous years I can't remember them having this trouble. Each time they try to score, they miss. The ball either goes too wide, or too high and over the top. They just can't get it to go between the posts."

At this stage I was somewhat unsure whether I preferred having a sensible conversation with someone who knows what they are on about or trying to have a sensible conversation with someone who hasn't a clue what they're on about. So I stayed quiet. The lady put me in the picture.

She said: "I've made some enquiries, and apparently my team is getting caught out by the rules this year which say that all the teams have to use the new lightweight balls."

If you've never seen me speechless, you needed to be there.

MAD WORLD 35
HAPPY EMPLOYEES BUT NO TEA

I had a good one this morning. A chap stopped me in Penhurst for directions and when I looked at his invoice it said Penhurst, Kent. I said: "This is Sussex and you want Kent." He said: "No, I expect the Kent bit is wrong and I want Penhurst." So I told him: "No, I think you will find the Kent bit is right and it is the 'S' that is missing from Penshurst, that's what's wrong. So I suggest you had better phone your office."

A few years ago, we were told at work that our employer had decided to make a small amount of money available to each office for the employees to spend on improving their working environment, thus creating happy employees. Suggestions were called for, but many were a complete waste of time as we don't need a telly in the rest room or a snooker table. We would never use them as we don't get tea breaks or lunch breaks. We drink our tea while sorting and eat our meals while driving. The only idea that got the popular vote was a Christmas do. Not my vote of course. So, those who went to the do, did. And those of us who didn't, got vouchers. That system worked OK the first year so naturally it got changed the following year. Unfortunately, most of the office had realised from their previous experience, that perhaps my angle on the situation was right. If we can't stand the sight of each other at 4.30 am then why the hell would we want to socialise at 9.30 pm? So, when the notice went up on the board for people to put their names down for the Christmas do, only about 4 names were entered. Everyone else said they would prefer vouchers. With the coach already booked, it caused quite a headache for Mr. Punch, our manager. But he's not as silly as he looks. He couldn't possibly be. He waved his stick and said, "There will be no vouchers this year and so all those not going on the bus will get nothing". Bingo. He filled his bus overnight. So those that went on the bus went to the dogs. I couldn't have put it better myself. In Brighton, to be precise. And those of us that didn't, got nothing.

Then the company decided that we were missing the point and that the money was supposed to be spent within the boundary of the office and not up the road on food and drink. They wanted happy employees. Not incredibly happy employees. Suggestions were called for again. One suggestion, from a rather feminine chap who lives in the woods, was hanging baskets. Oh yes, I can really see me leaping out of bed at 3.30 am to rush to work to see how our hanging baskets are doing. We packed him off back to the woods with a bag of nuts. How about a pressure washer? That was the next suggestion. Great. I've got the dirtiest round in the office so a couple of quick squirts with that each week would be just the job. Trouble was, someone clobbered it with a van before I got to use it and didn't tell anyone. I connected it up to the water supply, plugged it into the mains, switched it on and cleaned half the van when bang, flash, the fuse box in the office had gone and all the lights went out. So we were banned from using it.

More ideas required. No one was brave enough to suggest a year's supply of gob stoppers for Mr. Punch so we ended up with free tea. We had always previously paid for our tea but, for the first time ever, we could have our tea for free and there was to be coffee for those who wanted it. Two cups a day as well. And if you worked on your day off, it was even better value. Alas, 6 months later we arrive at today.

Mr. Punch was waiting on the door step this morning. Must be bad. He only ever comes to work if there's bad news. The rest of the time he stays in bed getting his much needed beauty sleep. He leaves us to do all the work. We were called to a meeting and waited while he prepared his notes ready for his big speech. He puffed out his immense chest.

"There is to be no more free tea." he boomed, "You will have to start paying for it again."

"That's the way to do it." I thought I heard him say under his breath.

Oh dear, I thought, we must have been clobbered again by the regulator for all our good work and now there's to be a whip round to pay the fine. One of my braver colleagues decided to question this decision.

"Why?" he asked.

"Because," said Mr. Punch, "if the company gives you tea and it is free then it becomes a taxable benefit." Well, I'm off for my medication now, bye.

MAD WORLD 36
DID YOU SEE THAT?

The idiots at No: 23 have been at it again.
   A couple of my bikes are fitted with alarms and I hate alarms. One of these bikes, a Triumph, has had a dodgy battery for the last year or so and has been unreliable at holding its charge. It is my fear of alarms that has dissuaded me from trying to fit a new battery. One morning during this past week, I got it out of the garage to ride to work and it wouldn't start. My patience ran out. I don't have a lot of patience with faulty machinery and expect a high standard of behaviour from all my bikes and cars.
   I could see a free weekend coming up, so I bought a new battery in readiness for fitting it on Sunday morning.
   I had a good read of the alarm's instruction manual to ensure that I knew how to disable the alarm before disconnecting the battery.
   After a slow start to the day, I went into the garage to change the battery on the Triumph.
   Jayne, meanwhile, decided to have a bath.

   Garage: Having disabled the alarm, I removed the seat, side panel and various other bits and bobs and proceeded to disconnect the battery. As I removed the wires from the first battery terminal the alarm went off. It made a hell of a din. No matter how many times I hit the relevant buttons on the key fob it just wouldn't stop. The only way to restore peace and quiet to the street on this Sunday morning, and to stop people looking at No: 23, was to reconnect the wires to the battery terminal and think again.

Indoors: Jayne emerges from the bathroom naked and, upon walking up the hall, sees Oliver the cat sitting on a windowsill. Jayne decides to spend a moment looking through the net curtain at the world outside whilst stroking Oliver, before finding some clothes to put on. All of a sudden, an alarm goes off in the garage, Oliver turns his head 180 degrees to see where the noise is coming from, the net curtain catches on his ear and goes with him and the neighbours get a treat. The advantages of living where we are, surrounded by elderly neighbours are a) they have poor eyesight and b) if they did see anything, they have short memories.

MAD WORLD 37
ATTIRE OR A TYRE?

One of the best comments I've heard during this unbearably hot weather was Jayne looking at our open fireplace and saying:
"I can't imagine ever being cold enough again to want to light the fire."

Having not had a day off for a couple of months and with temperatures reaching record levels, I can't help but get a bit tired which can, perhaps, account for some unusual goings-on.

There have been the predictable stupid questions from customers such as:
"Steve, have you got air conditioning in your van?"

There have been the amusing comments from customers like:
"I don't like this hot weather. What I would like to see is a good frost."

And having had my August haircut a couple of weeks early due to an impending wedding job with one of my cars, I was asked by a particularly buxom lady:
"Steve, you've obviously had your annual trim [annual?], does having your hair cut take all your strength?"

To which I replied:
"I'm not answering that. I'm going to leave you wondering."

I arrived at a property the other day and was met by the gentleman of the house. He leant against his car as we started chatting.

Gent: "Do you have to wear a tie in this hot weather?"

Me: "I don't have to wear a tie at all, ever, while at work and I'm actually the only one who does."
Gent: "It looks jolly smart with that shirt."
At this point the lady of the house, the gent's wife, appeared.
Me: "My boots see a bit of polish from time to time which is also unusual where I work."
Gent: "You must be swimming against the tide."
I turned to his wife.
Me: "Hello, sorry to ignore you but we were in a deep discussion."
Gent: "Yes, we were discussing attire."
Wife: "A tyre?"
Gent: "Yes, attire."
Lady wife turns to me and asks,
Wife: "You were discussing a tyre?"
Realising we were leaning against the car and the obvious confusion this had caused I tried to put things right.
Me: "No, not a tyre," I said, pointing to the wheel of the car, "Attire," I told her, pointing to myself.
Wife: "Oh, clothes, why didn't you just say clothes?"
Me: "But I didn't say it, well what I mean is it wasn't me who didn't say it, it was him who didn't say it. And I didn't realise that talking to him would get me into so much trouble."
Wife: "Oh, he's so old fashioned. He's so old fashioned, that when he talks, he talks like a really old book."
I felt this to be unjust.
Me: "Oi, Piss Off."
Gent: "Crikey, you've got courage to say that to my wife. I've never had the courage to say that to her."

I had another episode when delivering to a property on a Monday, which should have been my day off. I walked into the kitchen where there were about 8 or more people sitting having their elevenses.

The lady of the house greeted me with:
"Oh no, you haven't brought us another whole load of trouble have you?"

Turning straight around with the items still in my hand I walked back towards the door saying:
"I give up my day off to come here for you and that's what I get in return."

As I reached the back door I spotted the bin with the lid half open. I raised my arm towards the ceiling and said "There you go," threw the whole lot straight in to the bin and walked out.

MAD WORLD 38
THE REVENUE SAYS HAVE A CUPPA

Remember the episode of the free tea being withdrawn by my employer due to it being a taxable benefit?

Well, one of the readers of these Mad Worlds happens to be a successful accountant who emailed me over a copy of the rules on meals and refreshments taken from the official Inland Revenue website. We are entitled to a cuppa. I then printed off a copy for my Boss who, it appears, did nothing with it. Or was told from above to do nothing with it.

My Boss, Five Bellies, is away on holiday for 3 weeks. I believe he has gone abroad due to the invention of double decker planes which enables him to have one floor and the other passengers can travel too, on the other floor.

His replacement is a chap we've seen many times and who we affectionately call Bare Minimum Bob, due to the enormous workload he doesn't do. He had reason to mention the taxable tea during our weekly worktime waste time meeting.

I took great pleasure in being able to put him in the picture regarding this matter as I happened to have a copy of the Inland Revenue rules in my locker.

As I left the office to begin my delivery, I noticed Bare Minimum Bob on the office computer, on the Inland Revenue website checking my information.

I puzzled over this for an hour. Could we really have someone on our side for a change? Someone who was actually going to do something for us?

Then I remembered the affectionate name they have for Bob at another office: Kenco.

Because he always has a cup of coffee in his hand.

Also this week: I sorted up a letter from abroad to an address in the town which went something like this:
Mr. Kevin Smith
01xxx 72xxxx
East Sussex,
England.

All we had to do was ring the chap up and ask him where he lived.

While I think about it. I took my co-driver, Jayne, around Eastbourne on a recce for a wedding we were going to do for someone so that she could learn the route. We were traveling along the road and had a conversation that went like this:

Me: "Now, we aren't going to take the first left, here, but the second left...........here."

Co-Driver Jayne: "Oh yes, I see. The road where the house on the corner has scaffolding around it."

Me: "No, the road opposite the pub. The scaffolding may not be there in a week's time."

MAD WORLD 39
A PAIN IN THE CHEST (INSTEAD OF THE NECK)

A couple of weeks ago, we were watching television on Saturday evening when Jayne said she had a pain in her chest. Seeing this as being, possibly, one of the signs that my therapist had told me to look out for as an indication that Jayne was in the mood, I asked:
"Would you like me to take a look at your chest?"
"Definitely not." came the reply.
"Shame, in that case it's obviously indigestion so I expect it'll be fine in the morning and I'm off to bed." I told her.
Sure enough, everything was fine by the morning but, out of pure spite, Jayne decided to make an appointment with her Doctor so that she could show him her chest. And she made the appointment for when I was at work.
When she showed her Doctor where it had hurt, not where it hurts please note, but where it used to hurt, he said:
"I would like my mate at the Hospital to have a look at this, or these, so I'll give you 2 weeks off work so you are free to see him whenever he can fit you in."
By the time she got home, the phone was ringing and the Hospital were asking: "How soon can you come? Next Wednesday?"
Not to be outdone, I got my round done in record time and went with her to the Hospital. We allowed an hour and ten minutes to get there and made it in 35. If we had allowed 35 minutes........
Well, we were nice and early and spent the first hour doing the usual: Reading all the notices a couple of dozen

times. Sitting on the edge of our seats each time a man in a white coat appeared to collect his next patient. Wondering why the chap who arrived just five minutes ago had already gone in. Then two young looking, healthy looking, happy looking Doctors appeared and called for Jayne.
"Would you like me to come?" I enquired.
"No thank you." I was told. And off she went. I had to amuse myself with the floor show going on around me.

There was a great big lady receptionist who had been eating an enormous packet of crisps for the last 20 minutes. Chomp.....Chomp.....Chomp she had been going and each time the phone rang she speeded up...Chomp-Chomp-Chomp-Chomp "Hello can I help you?"

Then she spent another ten minutes cleaning her computer and key board so as to destroy the evidence. She then spotted a little old lady sitting in a company issue NHS wheelchair just in front of me. The lady receptionist came toddling over and asked the little old lady:

"You've been sitting there a long time, are you waiting for transport?"

"Sorry?" The little old lady replied.

"Are you waiting for transport?" the receptionist asked again, raising her voice as she did so.

"Oh, yes." Was the little old lady's answer.

The receptionist toddled back to her office saying she would get on to them and went into her little booth and made a phone call. Then out she came again and went over to the little old lady.

"Your transport will be about 15 minutes." she told her. The look on her face was a picture when the little old lady replied:

"Oh it will be a lot longer than that. My daughter said she would pick me up after she has done her shopping and she shops for a month you know."

The receptionist toddled off and made another phone call.

Jayne returned, looking rather too happy and said we had to wait for her results. Unable to cope with all this I said:
"I'm off to see my old mate who has just had a big operation on her leg. You can come and find us when you've finished here."
"Which ward is she in?" Jayne enquired.
"I can't remember the name, but it's a double barrelled name and I've seen it written on the wall." I told her as I departed.
I found my 80 year old mate, who had just had a big operation on a leg which had proved troublesome and who now had a couple of replacement knee caps. Perhaps one replacement would have been enough for one leg? She looked a bit rough, as you can imagine just 2 days after the operation. She had a blood pressure armband on her right arm and a half empty bag of blood going into her left arm. She said the ingoing blood was due to finish in 3 hours.
All of a sudden the blood pressure armband pumped up tight and blood spurted out of the left arm where it was supposed to be going in. It was like a little red fountain.
"Look at that, I've never seen that before." I said.
"Oh no, what do you think has happened now?" my friend asked.
"I expect you're full up," I replied, "I'll go and get a Nurse to switch it off."
Jayne turned up, took one look and had to go back outside. Good, that wiped the smile off her face. I bid farewell to my friend and on the way back to the car I was informed that there is more than one ward with a double barrelled name and Jayne had found them all. Blast. That wiped the smile off my face.

MAD WORLD 40
FIVE BELLIES, WHAT DOES HE DO?

After two and a half weeks back at work following my holiday, I have finally found something to smile about. Maybe it's just my view of things but at least my day at work was a bit more manageable after the last two awful weeks.

I know I've had my fair share of sick leave over the years what with migraines and back pain, and my goolies are legendary. But some of the sick leave in the office is becoming rather suspect.

Fair enough, we do have one gormless chap off for another couple of months. After breaking his hand he managed to put his other hand through a plate glass window, severing tendons and almost losing the hand. Bet the jobs his Mum has to do for him right now are jobs she thought she'd seen the back of 20 years ago. At least from his point of view it proves us wrong with what we've all been saying about him since he started. He couldn't possibly do 'that' with both hands in a bandage.

But this morning we had two more people phone in sick. The first chap is a chap who only ever works a few days a week. Trouble is, we never know which days he'll be in. Here we are, Thursday, and it was his second day off sick this week. Apparently he has panic attacks. Unfortunately for us he gets them at 3.30 am when his alarm goes off. I get mine when I open my wage slip.

   When someone goes sick we have to split a delivery up as we don't have spare men. Or women. When the shout goes up: "Who wants to do some extra?" those with 6 kids, a wife and a mistress to support, put their hands up while the rest of us look on in amazement. The delivery is then done, hopefully, on overtime.

   The second chap to phone in sick this morning was Five Bellies himself, the Manager. He really was too ill to sit on his chair at work. One wag in the office suggested we could split Five Bellies duties up between us and we could do his work and claim the overtime. After much excitement, the office went quiet. Nobody could think what Five Bellies actually does. The company might be happy to pay him for doing nothing but surely we would be for it if we claimed overtime for doing nothing. What a pity. Now for the sting in the tail. It brought the house down. Five Bellies lives on a round that is delivered to by us. How pleased we were to find ourselves sorting out birthday cards for Mrs. Five Bellies. How lucky she was to have him at home on her birthday.

MAD WORLD 41
LEAVE THE LIGHT ON FOR THE BURGLAR

Here we go again. I'm sorry, but this has left my head spinning. Like everyone that gets these Mad World emails, I just work hard to get the things I want in life. Perhaps I have been working too hard lately.

Yesterday, Sunday, Jayne and I came up with the idea of getting another compost bin to go with the 2 we already have. We might also get another water butt to go with the 2 we already have. We managed to get through last summer without using any water from the tap to put on the garden. Trying to do our bit for the environment. We recycle all our paper, tins, bottles and plastics. Jayne said she would like to go a step further with the environmental theme and had picked up a leaflet giving details on grants towards things like property insulation and solar panels for heating etc. We could only have a grant if we were over 60 years of age or have a child under 16 years of age or are on benefits. So, because we just work hard, we have to pay the full whack for everything.

Then last night on the television we watched the news and heard: No more room in the prisons for the criminals. Might have to start filling up the police stations with all the crooks.

Today it all got too much and I'm afraid I let my attitude get the better of me. A chap was telling me that he had dug an inspection pit in his workshop so as to make working on lorries a lot easier. What a good idea. The chap had the man from the Health and Safety department come around to sign it off as safe for use. All was well but the Health and Safety man warned my friend that he must leave a light on all night in the pit in case a burglar fell in and hurt himself. In disbelief I said: "You don't have to leave him a flask of tea as well do you?"

MAD WORLD 42: WHERE'S MY DINNER GONE?

This one does have a happy ending, so stick with it. But first of all, I'll give you a bit of background info to help you along the way. My partner, Jayne, hates going shopping. For anything. She used to be able to leave home, travel to the local supermarket, do a week's grocery shopping, return home again and have it all away in the cupboards within the hour. Jayne must have been the fastest thing you've ever seen in a supermarket. Now we have a computer, the groceries are often ordered on line and delivered straight to the door.

We tend to live in properties which are half way up, or down, a hill. I dislike the tops of hills as the view can be nice but the wind is awful. I dislike the bottom of hills due to the threat of global warming and higher sea levels. Half way up a hill is also jolly handy for bump starting vehicles that have a petrol engine. We live on a right hand corner half way down the hill.

Now for the little tale of yesterday afternoon.

I returned home from work to find a message on the phone from Jayne. She was telling me not to turn the oven on tonight as we had run out of chips and, unless the shopping arrived early, we would have to have potatoes with our evening meal. The shopping was due between 6 pm and 7 pm. At twenty to six, the doorbell went. I answered the door to discover a chap who was getting on in years standing there on the doorstep. I thought it must have been another collection for Help the Aged.

"Good evening, Sir," he said, "I've got your groceries. I'm a bit early, but is it alright to deliver?" He asked.

"Certainly." I replied, as he went back along the drive and out to his van which was parked on the corner facing down the hill. Meanwhile, I went into the kitchen to turn the oven on. Oh yes, I'm a real wiz in the kitchen these days, I know where all the switches are. Things were looking hopeful. The driver returned and deposited the first load into our porch and departed once more for his van. At this point I decided, as usual, to go out to his van to help him with the next load. As I walked along the drive I couldn't believe my eyes. The Supermarket van was going down the hill with the driver chasing after it. The steering lock must have been locked with the wheels turned slightly to the right as the van was making its way across the road as it went. I've watched plenty of television programmes about some foreign countries where the locals sometimes chase their dinner around a field. Here was a chap chasing my dinner down the road. And what a fine job he was doing too. He might have been getting on in years and past the first flush of youth but boy could he run. His little old legs were a treat to watch. He was making good progress and got alongside the van as it mounted the pavement on the other side of the road and headed for someone's driveway. Unfortunately, the driveway it was heading towards is probably the shortest in the street and would be classed as a hardstanding for cars in front of the garage. Any chance he had of reaching the driver's door and getting the brake on was now looking pretty slim, but he refused to give up. I could see how the thought of spending the rest of his days having to live off just a state pension had instilled him with enormous enthusiasm for catching the van. The van started to go up the drive and, as the driver ran past the brick pillar, his luck ran out. The rear corner of the van caught the brick pillar and, as it fell, it caught the driver who then dropped to the ground with one of his feet going under the rear wheel as the van went past. It all seemed to happen in slow motion until there was a loud bang as the van buried itself in the garage door and came to a stop. The driver was lying under a pile of rubble. Never mind. Now for the happy ending.

The driver had left the rear doors open when he had set off in hot pursuit of the van so I was able to climb in the back and get my chips.

MAD WORLD 43
THE IMPORTANT CHRISTMAS CARDS

Season's Greetings to you all.

It's a busy time for all of us so I'll keep this short but I thought this was worth sharing.

As usual this year, I got well ahead with writing my Christmas cards and over the past week I've posted or delivered most of them. I have many people on the delivery that I like to give a Christmas card to and, a few get a Rolls-Royce or Bentley one. Various doors have opened throughout the week with people coming out to thank me for their card. One instance will stay with me for a very long time. The door opened as I got to the letterbox and I was greeted by the lady of the house saying: "Thank you, thank you for your lovely Christmas card, come and see where I have put it."

I followed the lady into the house whereupon she pointed to a small table where I could see my Christmas card displayed along with one other.

"Look, look," she said with delight, pointing to the table in the corner.

"It's on the table there. That's where I put all my special cards. The card on the left is from the Archbishop of Canterbury, written in his own hand, and the card on the right is yours."

Beat That! No doubt all she is waiting for is a card from the Queen and she'll have the full set.

MAD WORLD 44
THE OUTLAWS COME TO DINNER. CHRISTMAS 2006

I had an interesting conversation today with the Mother of a Bride who I took to her daughter's wedding this year. The Mother of the Bride informed me that this year had been the best year of her life and the good thing about it was that I had been a part of it. I suggested to her that the good thing for me was that I had managed to be a part of it without actually having to marry her daughter.

Well that was Christmas. Christmas 2006. How was it for you?

For the first time in 8 years at the bungalow, we thought we would risk inviting Jayne's parents for Christmas dinner. We had calculated that they would spend most of the morning visiting one of Jayne's brothers who lives locally with a couple of dozen kids and we also knew they had been invited out to tea. So, as long as the tea invite didn't fall through, we should be safe. Other precautions we had taken were: Jayne had the 23rd and the 24th off so as to prepare, mentally. We would both have Boxing Day to recover and I also had Sunday 24th off due to the high wages it takes these days to get me to work on a Sunday. The first Christmas Eve I've had off in about 20 years. With a view to saving the best till last, I'll tell you how it all went but not in chronological order.

With everything cooking nicely, I decided that with the visitors due to arrive shortly, I couldn't get away with disappearing into the garage for an hour on this occasion.

So I helped in the kitchen instead. All the veg had been in for a while when I spotted the parsnip Jayne's Mum likes so much with her Christmas dinner, sitting on the side. You have never seen a vegetable peeled, cut and in the oven so fast in all your life.

We had a pre-arranged plan to let Jayne's father open the bottle of wine while we were busy in the kitchen. Although he'd had a couple of beers before leaving home and a glass of sherry when he got to us, he had a problem with the wine. The thought of having to share the bottle had made him shake and instead of the cork coming out with a pop, it came out in bits with most of it going back into the bottle.
"Do you have a tea strainer?" the kitchen staff were asked.
We looked at each other knowing we had one but where had we last seen it? Outside. It was last used for getting the slugs out of the Slug Pubs in the garden.
"Shall I get it?" I asked.
The look on Jayne's face gave me the answer so I quickly asked if she had a flour sieve. All manner of pots and pans came flying out of a cupboard followed by a dusty sieve. Great. Didn't bother rinsing it as alcohol is supposed to be good at killing germs.

As we appear to be poor company on these occasions, Jayne's parents had a couple of dozen phone calls on their mobile phones from their grandchildren who are scattered all over the country. I found this irritating. Actually, I thought it rude. I considered giving them my: you should cover the ends of your mobile phones in Vaseline*, but as it was Christmas, I was a little more restrained and merely suggested that if I had a mobile phone that rang as much as theirs did I felt sure I would have to throw it in the bin. I was told to get with it. Perhaps another time we shall have to play charades. Perhaps we already were.

But my favourite moment from Christmas Day? Ten minutes before our guests were due to arrive, Jayne had one last check around the bungalow to make sure we were ready. She came down the hall saying, "Stephen, the hinges on the toilet seat have broken."
GREAT.
That will test her Mums sense of balance.

*When someone is irritating me with the overly enthusiastic use of a camera, video recorder or, in this case, a mobile phone, I usually suggest they cover the end of it in Vaseline as then it won't be quite so painful when I shove it up their.........

There is one last thing that I shall always remember from that Christmas. I usually attend the old folk's lunch at Christmas and this year I found myself sitting next to the oldest man in the village. He will be 93 in a couple of months. I don't like sprouts and so, as I passed the bowl of sprouts over to him, I said, "I'm going to give these a miss but it will be OK for you to have some because you are allowed to fart as you live on your own."
He replied: "I've got my neighbours to think of you know."

MAD WORLD 45
ANOTHER BREAKDOWN

HAPPY NEW YEAR TO YOU ALL.

Another bad day at the office.

Following the return of my van after a colleague got stuck in one gear and then burnt the clutch out, I have now experienced once more the top quality that is the Vauxhall Combi van. I arrived at a call and, upon opening my door, heard a loud bang. I looked all around the van and everything looked fine. The door still worked and the window still went up and down. I made my delivery and continued to the next call. I made the delivery, got back into the van and went to close the door. That was the turning point of my day I suppose. My driver's door was locked solid in the wide open position. The door check strap had broken and had now wedged the door open. If you don't catch the door on a windy day, the check strap should stop it flying back and bouncing off the front wing.

It has always been my policy to try and break down at a call where tea and biscuits are available on a bad day or tea and cake on a good day. I asked to use the phone and after telling my mate, the PHG, about my good fortune, he said he would contact the workshop. The lady of the house then offered me tea, as planned, so yes, please. The lady of the house then told me I would have to have it black as she had run out of milk so.....no, thank you.

Look, I told you at the start it was a bad day. Even I get it wrong sometimes.

As the lady of the house stood puffing on her cigarette she asked if I would like to bring my sandwiches into the kitchen and sit in the warm while I waited for the mechanic to arrive. OK, so I failed here as well with my reply.

"No, thank you, it's too smoky in here for me, so I'll wait outside in the van."

So there I was, sitting in my van having lunch with the door wide open, and I get a call to the phone. We have 3 mechanics, or rather one mechanic and two grease monkeys who take it in turns to work at our local workshop. Surely the odds had to be better than the lottery.

I picked up the phone and said, "Hello."

"Hello. Steve." came the reply.

I spoke without thinking, impulse I suppose, I've never been any good at hiding my disappointment when other members of the population don't quite come up to my expectations.

"OH, NO."

"Now look here, do you want me to come out or not?" The grease monkey asked.

"Yes, please." I told him, as I went on to give him directions. I was as far from my office as I could be and he was another quarter of an hour beyond that. I usually reckon on waiting an hour from phoning until someone arrives.

"That sounds complicated to me." the grease monkey said as if he was changing his mind about coming.

"No, no, no," I told him, "you only have to turn right twice after leaving town and you'll find me. You just have to make sure you turn right at the right time."

Well, he did turn up, I finished the round and then went to the workshop and had a new check strap fitted. I booked three hours overtime to make myself feel better about it and, as that hadn't worked, came home and got my axe out and chopped some logs in half. The pain in my tennis elbow then took my mind off the breakdown of my van.

Today I asked my Manager, Five Bellies, if he had heard about my troubles yesterday.

"Oh, yes," he said, "I heard your check strap broke and your door got jammed open."

Then he continued, "No trouble getting in and out of the van then."

I love my job.

Also today, Five Bellies asked me if I had a spare peaked cap like the one I wear when it rains? He told me that a local amateur dramatics group had asked him if he could lend them a cap for a production they're doing. I was the only person he could think of that still has a proper cap as we can no longer get them. Yes, I do have a spare so I lent it to him.

I asked Five Bellies why the amateur dramatics group couldn't just have one of the baseball caps that replaced the peaked cap. The amateur dramatics society had told him that a baseball cap wouldn't do. I'm sure there's a moral in there somewhere.

MAD WORLD 46
PASSING OUT

I haven't written lately as I didn't think anything had happened that was worthy of note. Apparently, something did happen, but I missed it. And yes, the lady concerned is OK and back at work.

As in most occupations, other than jockeys, our employees come in a variety of shapes and sizes. One of our ladies has quite generous proportions after eating too many generous portions. I was told on Saturday that after I had left the office on Friday morning, this particular lady had passed out. She had gone spark out, hitting the wooden floor with a hefty 'donk.' This is unusual for a Friday as the wage slips arrive on a Thursday.

Obviously, this resulted in an ambulance being called and some overtime becoming available for those who wanted it. So, not all bad news after all.

When hearing of the excitement that I'd missed, I asked what I thought was an obvious question: "Did anyone try rubbing her chest?"

A male colleague replied with, "Steve, I don't think that's the answer to everything." Worth a try though, surely?

A female colleague replied with, "Steve, that's why I'm the First Aider and you are not."

I always thought the idea of First Aid was to take the victim's mind off of their problems.

The female First Aider then went on, so the whole office could hear: "In fact, I can't imagine anything that would make you get up faster than opening your eyes and seeing Big Steve standing over you."

MAD WORLD 47
HE'S IN THE ARMY NOW. OR MAYBE NOT

I know there are some subjects that wouldn't normally come under the heading of 'humorous' and I'm very aware of the serious side to this one.

I had an interesting chat with a lady last Friday as she told me that her son was going for an interview on the following Monday at the local Army Recruitment Office. I enquired as to what the day involved for her boy and she told me he would have an interview and then undergo various tests so that he could be assessed with a view as to which Army Corps he would be most suited to. I asked the lady which part of the Army her son was most hopeful of getting into and she told me he fancied the Communications Corps.

This week I've been keen to speak to the lady again to hear how her son got on with his big day. Today, Friday, I saw the lady in question and I asked her how it all went.

The concerned mother told me: "We got the day wrong, it wasn't last Monday but next Monday. They told us we were a week early."

I replied: "I think he may have blown his chances for the Intelligence Corps."

I think he may not be suited for Communications either, do you?

MAD WORLD 48
100 YEAR OLD LADIES KNOW HOW TO HAVE FUN

Today I've taken a 100 year old lady to her birthday luncheon. Nothing unusual in that but it's the way in which we have got to this point that has left us a bit stunned this week. We feel we should share this with you.

Less than 3 months ago, I was recommended to a family who were looking for someone to provide transport for their grandmother to go to her 100th birthday. That was a great success and she really enjoyed her ride in the Rolls. Two weeks ago, the same family rang up to say they had another 100 year old lady wanting to go to a birthday do. Surely this could only happen in our town. A bit like buses, wait all year for one to come along and then.........

The Rolls is away so it had to be the Bentley. It turns out the two 100 year old ladies live in the same block of flats.

Six days ago, the 2nd 100 year old lady set her bedroom alight, walked out and shut the door and got a neighbour to phone the fire brigade. While they were on the way, a bottle of perfume in the bedroom exploded and blew the entire window out onto the front lawn without even breaking the glass. The whole block was evacuated for several hours. On their return and, without accommodation for the night, the 2nd 100 year old lady had a sleep over with the old girl I had met 3 months previously. For the remainder of the week she has been in a local Nursing Home. All this became front page news in the local *Observer*.

Now I know I have always said that I only seem to appeal to women who are either over 80 or in a wheelchair or both, but I hadn't realised I had cornered the market in 100 year olds. Mind you, this latest was a Miss, so I either had to be in with a chance or she's spent 100 years batting for the other side.

My preparations for all this? On Friday morning, while out on delivery, I had delivered to a farm and was returning to my van when I stepped onto a drain cover/manhole cover. No doubt we have all stepped onto a few of those in our time and thought nothing of it. I was walking quite quickly, as required by my employer, and as I stepped onto the drain cover my foot went straight through it. Maybe our new digital bathroom scales don't lie after all. With one leg down the drain, my body slammed into the brick paving incredibly hard. If I had banged my head I feel sure I would have been knocked out. With pain coursing throughout my body, I got back into the van and returned to the office, unsure as to whether I would be able to continue the deliveries. After a quick inspection of the painful parts, I discovered only one knee was leaking (bleeding) slightly so went back out and completed the deliveries.

On my return to the office, I got my mate the PHG to do an accident report. This is no longer in book form but is done on the computer. PHG entered my name and employee number and that was as far as the computer would let him go. Big red lettering across the screen stated: Not a recognised employee. And, in a fortnight's time, I am to be issued with a certificate showing my 20 years' service to the company.

After soaking in a hot bath, I managed to go to work again on Saturday but was a bit uncomfortable in a few places. Yes, it was another case of, "Oh, balls. Now look what's happened."

Five Bellies, the Governor, was at work on Saturday and I asked him if PHG had told him we had tried to complete an accident report and the computer wouldn't do it.

Five Bellies answered "No."

In my ignorance I would have thought the delivery office manager would have gone on to enquire as to what had happened. In my frustration, if any of you would like to read the letter that I will be handing in to my boss on Monday morning, you can send your request to me by email and I'll send you a copy back on email as I wrote it on the computer.

Has anyone got any ideas as to how I could just lead a quiet life?

We all seem to be rushing through life in such a hurry to do things and yet, I've noticed these 100 year old ladies trundle along as if they've got all the time in the world.

MAD WORLD 49
IT'S A TEAPOT

OK, so it's not so Mad World this one but it was very funny at the time.

I haven't had many colleagues over the years who I would class as mates that I would want to socialise with. One of my few friends from work has just mentioned that it's about time Jayne and I paid him and his young family a visit for a cup of tea. This reminded me of the first time we visited about 2 years ago. Don't worry, we're accustomed to not being invited back so two years between visits didn't seem unusual to us. I think the long delay was also made worse by the fact that I pulled his leg a bit after our last visit and told him that I fancied his wife. Some people just can't tell when I'm joking and unfortunately, this had a detrimental effect on our relationship. For 2 years, so it would seem.

Anyway, prior to our first visit, I had told my friend that I would fill his drive with a Rolls-Royce when we came round so that I could give him a ride up the road in it. He then spent a couple of weeks trying to convince his lovely wife that I was a bit unusual compared to their normal circle of friends. I don't think that could have been easy as I have always considered myself to be fairly normal. I can only guess that perhaps he doesn't have many friends who visit in a Rolls-Royce. They must leave theirs at home.

The big day came and we parked the Rolls on his drive, and halfway across the pavement as well, I seem to recall. Our visit also coincided with me being almost ready for my spring trim. You could see that my autumn trim had been a long time ago. It was always much more cost effective back then to only be splashing out 3 quid twice a year instead of these days when the wedding jobs send me running to the scissor lady more often than I'd like.

We were invited in and sat at the dining table which was resplendent with the best china including a cake stand filled with Mr. Kipling's finest. Two of my friend's three boys were present and all was going well until the eldest son, a 9 year old, arrived a bit late on parade after having been across the road playing with his friend. We were all sitting around the table eating the cake and drinking the tea and the 9 year old sat down opposite me. And he stared. I felt a bit uncomfortable about this but there was nothing I could do but stare back. He looked amazed. I felt like the main attraction in a freak show. I don't know if he had never seen a ginger beard before or whether he liked the look of my woolly hat.

He was given a china plate and offered a cake from the cake stand which he took and then it all went a bit wrong for our hosts, my mate and his truly lovely wife. The little 9 year old boy pointed to the tea pot, proudly sitting on a mat in the middle of the table, and asked his Mum: "What's that?"

"It's a teapot." his Mum replied.

"Oh," said the little boy, "What's it for?"

Brilliant.

I could hear my mate quietly choking on his almond slice and out of the corner of my eye, I could see his lovely wife slowly disappearing beneath the end of the table. The poor little chap had managed to live 9 years without ever seeing a teapot.

Modern Living.

I have been doing these Mad World ramblings for about a year now and we have reached No: 50. I find this amazing. I know it isn't possible for everyone to enjoy every Mad World that comes along but as long as you enjoy some of them that makes it worthwhile. I still enjoy writing and, at times, I find it therapeutic.

To mark the achievement of reaching No: 50, I hope you'll excuse my choice of subject. I've tried to behave myself up until now but I am feeling the need to get this one out of my system. March represents my 20th year in the job and I would like to share with you some tales from my dim and distant past. I think this one comes loosely under the heading of hanky-panky.

I hope it doesn't cause too many of you to cancel your subscription.

MAD WORLD 50
SLIGHTLY NAUGHTY AT 50

Jayne and I have always tried to support as many village events as we can over the years and we both enjoy the friendships we have formed with a great many of the villagers. Evening events are difficult for me, especially if they are held mid-week. On the odd occasion that we have attended an evening event we are often asked by some of the elderly villagers if we could give them a lift home as they know we'll be leaving before the function has finished. It is with great respect that I would like to share with you a memory I have of an elderly chap who is no longer with us. Jayne and I were asked to run the gentleman and his wife home after the Harvest Supper one year. We always make a run for it when the hymn sheets come out because I have to be up so early the next morning. We gave the elderly couple a lift home and, as the wife skipped up the garden path to activate the outside light, we helped her husband get out of the car and steadied him on his walking sticks. He was in his early eighties and had worked hard all his life. Jayne asked him if there was anything else he would like her to do for him before she left.

His answer, with a twinkle in his eye, was superb:

"You can come and get me ready for bed if you like."

I knocked on a lady's door one day to ask if she would take a packet in for the elderly couple that lived next door.

With a wicked grin she said, "Yes, certainly, I expect it's their Viagra."

I thought this to be a tad uncalled for and wiped the smile of her face with:

"That I wouldn't know, but it's funny that you are able to recognise the packet."

I have often knocked on doors to get items signed for and been greeted by young ladies that have just got out of the bath or shower. They hold the towel that is wrapped around them and wonder how they can, at the same time, sign my bit of paper.

Ever helpful I suggest: "Don't worry, I'll hold the towel while you sign."

Many years ago I did every different round in the office before we went over to fixed duties. Back then, I would sometimes have my elevenses brought out to me by whoever I happened to be friendly with at the time. On one particularly wet and miserable Saturday morning, I was fortunate enough to be brought tea and cake by a young lady friend of mine. I was on a different delivery back then and so as to not block the lane, I parked the company van in the gateway to a field. The young lady parked her car across the front of the van but still in the lane. We sat in the car as I enjoyed my cup of tea and homemade buns. As I'm sure you'll understand, due to the heat from the tea, the windows had steamed up.

We saw a Police car drive past and then its brake lights came on and it reversed back up the lane. Out jumped PC Flatfoot, who had been given a Panda car to save his feet. He came and tapped on the window which I politely wound down.

"Excuse me Sir, we saw your van blocked-in and wanted to check that you're alright." he said.

"I'm fine," I said, "I'm just having my tea and cake. Would you like a cup?"

PC Flatfoot declined and went on his way.

We once had a chap working at our office who didn't manage to find himself a girl and get married until he was middle-aged. We all found it unsurprising that he'd struggled with the fairer sex as he had a reputation for being a bit odd. When he finally met the girl that went on to become his wife, his delight and enthusiasm were clear to see. His intended used to visit him out on his rounds. Hang on, where have I heard that before? They all start out as someone's intended.

Anyway, his enthusiasm got the better of them both one day when she visited him in a lane in a rural area. The two of them climbed in to the back of the van and shut the doors. When he returned to the office later in the day he was taken into the manager's office to be told, "We had a call from a member of the public this morning who said they saw you get in to the back of your van with a young lady and then close the doors. Said member of the public also mentioned that, after a short while, they had seen the van's suspension bouncing up and down."

In the sad environment that is our office, this particular chap had suddenly gained respect.

MAD WORLD 51
GOT TO HAVE A CUDDLE

Sorry I haven't been in touch with many of you for a while but things haven't been great of late so I've lost my sense of humour a bit. Operational changes at work haven't endeared the job to me. Nothing new there then. Gremlins in some of the motors at home have resulted in a tidy pile of bills on the sideboard waiting to be paid. I did consider selling a bike so as to steady the ship and placed one up for sale in a local motorbike shop. When Jayne came to give me a lift back home she mentioned that my bike was, in fact, the best looking bike in the showroom. I thought about this as I lay awake that night for 3 hours hoping no one would come into the shop the following day to buy it. I looked at the empty space in the garage in the morning and just had to have the bike back. I think I may be a lost cause. We do, however, seem to be turning the corner.

    I have a wedding job to do this Saturday and one of my colleagues will be doing the last bit of my round so that I can finish early. The bride I'm driving for this week doesn't know I'm coming so I will be a surprise. I hope she can take the shock. I got the job because the young couple I drove for last December got in touch a few weeks ago and said they had been so pleased with the service I had provided that they would like to treat their friends on their wedding day and pay for me to drive them in the Rolls. So, for the first time in my life, I am to be a wedding present. I think we could get into big trouble if we dwell on that thought for too long so....moving swiftly on:

    I have another positive thing on my mind this week. I've been approached by one of my nephews to see if I would drive him to his end of school Prom in a few months' time. He doesn't live locally so it won't be the easiest of jobs but I feel it could be quite an enjoyable one. He has hired me in the past when he was much younger and I was a lot cheaper. When he was about a year old I drove him to his christening in my first Rolls. It's good to see he has retained his taste for decent transport for a big occasion. However, it's unfortunate for him that my prices have gone up but he doesn't seem at all phased by that. Pocket money must be better these days or he may have saved the money he nearly spent on buying a company bike from me last year if you remember that.

I had a good day yesterday and found a couple of things to smile about. Thought I would share them with you.

My mate at work who has the three boys was telling me about his autistic son who is going to be in the Easter Play at the special school he attends. The young lad is about 9 years old and spends a lot of his time appearing to live in a world of his own. He is, however, quite intelligent and a proper little character. My mate was telling me that his son is going to be playing the part of Jesus and that the school had sent a letter home the other day to tell my mate and his wife: 'The school has never previously had a child who was so happy to be playing the part of Jesus and so pleased at the prospect of being crucified.'

Out on delivery, I called on a girl/lady who is about my age and, unfortunately for her, about my size. We have been great friends for many years. We have an agreement that if she is feeling a bit down, we have a big cuddle and if I am the one who's feeling rather down, we also have a big cuddle. In addition to this, if she has reason to celebrate, we also have a big cuddle and likewise, if I have cause for celebration we have a big cuddle. That just about covers most days of the week.

Yesterday, she opened the door as I arrived and asked: "Steve, can you do something for me?"

I immediately dashed indoors with her and we got into a big clinch and just as I was starting to think 'This isn't such a bad job after all, it definitely has some good moments,' the young lady said: "This wasn't what I had in mind today."

"Oh." I replied as I loosened my grip. She went on: "I have a letter to post and wondered if you could wait while I get a stamp."

I followed her into the kitchen where, being an old farmhouse type property, there is a very low beam running the whole length of the room. It's about eye height for me. Still in good spirits, I continued with the nonsense.

"I see," I said, "you lured me in here so that I would knock myself out. I'd be lying flat out on your kitchen floor and you'd have to phone for the ambulance."

She got me a cracker: "Oh I wouldn't bother. I would just step over you."

MAD WORLD 52
IT'S A HARLEY

Due to the prospect of having to send all the money I can lay my grubby little hands on to the Rolls-Royce garage in Goudhurst for the next 6 months, as has been the case for the last 6 months, I was beginning to think I might have to return to the good old bad old days when I used to service my bikes myself. I'm not too bad on 'the oil goes in there and comes out here bit,' but I needed to read up on what oil to put in which bike.

I've had a fair amount of stick over the past few years about having a Harley-Davidson in my collection and it is a bike that attracts a great deal of ridicule. I confess, not without reason. If you should ever have the experience of barrelling into a corner a bit too hot on a Harley, you'll really understand why the Americans build straight roads and limit the speed to 55mph. The Americans know they can't build motorcycles.

In a lot of people's eyes, a Harley is no more than a tractor. I think I may have found confirmation of this in the official Harley-Davidson handbook when I was looking up which oil to put in the engine. To quote from the book, 'If it is necessary to add oil and Harley-Davidson oil is not available, you can use an oil that's certified for diesel engines.'

While we're on the subject.

When I went looking to buy a Harley, we were in the dealer's showroom and he was explaining about all the different models [as if I didn't know] and he kept referring to the Fat Boy. After a while, Jayne looked at the dealer's belly and she looked at my belly and then she asked the chap: "What's a Fat Boy?"

It's not often I wish I'd gone on my own. The Fat Boy is the model name of the most popular bike they sell. See? The Americans have a sense of humour after all.

MAD WORLD 53
LET'S RECYCLE

'The Great Recycling Fiasco' announces the *local paper*. It can be a two hour wait when you join the queue for the local tip. Yes, indeed, our local Council and District Council have now considered it to be politically correct to join the big re-cycling drive. Up until now, they have been happy to just pay the fines and add it to our council tax. For some time we've had a green box for paper which has been collected fortnightly in addition to the weekly refuse collection. Now we have an additional black box for plastics and a black wheelie bin for refuse. Refuse collections are now fortnightly, alternating with paper and plastics every second week. Got it? Our neighbours in town have enough difficulty remembering what day of the week it is never mind which week we're in. The streets are littered with any combination of boxes and wheelie bins on any day of the week. And that's before we get issued with a brown wheelie bin for garden rubbish.

I felt sure the rural customers on my round would be much better at getting it right. My rural round had a new company take over the refuse collection and for a number of weeks half the village had no refuse collection at all. The new dustbin lorries were too big to go down the lanes. Maybe this is what put people out of sync. We now have two smaller lorries that go around the village, nose to tail, collecting the paper in one and plastics in the other. Then the following week another small lorry circulates collecting the refuse. Things were looking good on refuse day this week as I went around the village until I got to one particular household. It had obviously got a bit too much for one couple. As I drew up to their gate, I could see the wheelie bin, black box and green box all standing neatly in line.

A hand written sign announcing to the dustmen: "Take your pick."

MAD WORLD 54
DON'T GO UPSTAIRS

I've never been particularly good at sticking to the rules when out on my deliveries but I have one or two rules of my own which I try never to break. When entering a property to try and find someone for a signature, I wouldn't normally go upstairs. I think, however, I must have had a rush of blood to the head this week when trying to get a signature.

I arrived at a particular property that is way out in the woods. Judging by the car standing on the drive, I could see the husband had gone to work and the lady of the house must be in. I had an item that required a signature and I went through the lobby, through the kitchen and on through the dining room to the bottom of the stairs. It was Saturday morning and people are a pain to wake up on a Saturday. I started shouting and banging on the nearest door but got no reply.

I thought 'It's ridiculous that I should be standing here needing a signature and yet someone must be home.' I find these situations incredibly frustrating and, due to my annoyance, I climbed the stairs and discovered a bedroom door open. I peered in to discover the lady of the house asleep in bed. I started shouting and banging on the bedroom door. Still there was no response. Now, I know they like a bit of a drink at this particular house, so I went into the bedroom, and yes, I do know them well, and started shouting again. Each time I shouted, the lady rocked her head from side to side but still refused to wake up. What to do now? I didn't want to get too hands-on. Or two hands on, for that matter. 'What if she wakes up and sees me standing here?' I thought. 'She may ask me to jump in or she may think she has died and gone to heaven.' I gave up and returned to the dining room, signed for the item myself and put it on the table. For a bit of sport, maybe I should have signed for the item and put it on the bed. If she tells me this week that she had a dream about me the other night, I think I'll throttle her.

Going to such lengths for a signature reminded me of a colleague who knocked on a door one day to obtain a signature and the door was answered by a man who was having a heart attack. My colleague gave the gentleman the pen and bit of paper that required signing and said, "If you could just sign this, I'll call the ambulance."

MAD WORLD 55
IT'S THE WI

The rural community that I deliver to each day is spread over quite a wide area. Although it's a village, it has no real centre to speak of. No village shop or Post Office and no local school. There are one or two activities that take place in the village but over the last few years, quite a few people have moved into the village who tend to build a social life for themselves outside the village. We have a situation where many of the villagers don't know each other anymore. In fact, some people know very few people locally. Moves are afoot to form a new Women's Institute (WI). This could turn out to be the best thing to have happened in the village for years. From a personal point of view, I could also see other beneficial opportunities.

I set to and wrote a letter to 60 of the local lovelies and 2 more that live just outside the parish. I extolled the virtues of people in a village knowing each other. What a great opportunity it would be for the village if we could get people talking to each other again, I said. Please go along and join the WI. And the best bit? That'll be if our local WI does what several other WIs have done in the past. I can't wait till Christmas and they all strip off and make a calendar.

MAD WORLD 56
A JOB FOR THE BENTLEY

Still working under a bit of a cloud in my day job, I finally had something happen yesterday, a Sunday, which made me laugh. If you don't know the area where I live, you'll just have to use your imagination and I'll try to explain things as clearly as possible.

Whilst at my bank in town a couple of weeks ago, presumably to withdraw some money as I can't remember ever paying money in, I was asked by one of the chaps who works there whether I ever do driving jobs in my Rolls or Bentley. I told him that I sometimes do and asked what he had in mind. Sunday 8th July was to be a surprise Sunday dinner party at a local hotel for his aunt's 80th birthday. The aunt would need picking up from his Mum and Dad's house and the three of them would need taking all of 1/2 a mile down the road to the local hotel. I suggested that they would hardly have done their seatbelts up before they would be undoing them again. So, I suggested that we make something more of it and I'd collect them about half an hour beforehand and have a bit of a drive around, arriving at the hotel from the other direction. He thought this sounded like a good idea and the Rolls would be his preferred choice for the job. I emailed him some pictures of the Rolls and one of the Bentley, just for fun.

When I next visited the bank, he thanked me for the pictures and said his father thought the Bentley would be more suitable as the Rolls might look a bit too over the top if his neighbours were to see it parked on the drive. So I went off and did my recce and, in a gale force wind, washed and leathered the Bentley. What a pity he didn't want the Rolls as I'd already cleaned that, but never mind. Pickup at

12.30, arrive at the hotel at 1 pm, my route had been planned and timed, all set.

Sunday 8th July dawned a beautiful sunny day and I went to St. Leonards, to get the Bentley nice and early so as to beat the traffic. It looked lovely sitting on our drive. An hour before my departure time, the phone rang. It was the chap from the bank, just checking everything was OK and asking if I could do the pickup at 12.40 and arrive at the hotel at 12.55 please?

Here we go, I thought, bang goes my timed route. Back to the suck it and see method.

As I arrived at the pickup point, I could see the chap from the bank just up the road with his video camera. 'It's going to be one of those jobs,' I thought to myself. I so hate video cameras. I resisted the urge to give him a big wave as I got out of the car and just got on with the job of collecting my passengers. One aspect of doing a recce for jobs and working out the route is to establish which side of the car I need the women folk to sit. I always like to deposit them at their destination, either onto the pavement or as near as possible to the entrance to a venue. I don't like to unload long legged lovelies in skirts into the middle of the road. They can create a hazard and I like other road users to be concentrating on what they are doing as they go past my Rolls-Royce or Bentley. Once loaded up and where I wanted them, we set off up the road and I could see in my rear view mirror that we were being filmed as we disappeared into the distance.

I had the 80 year old lady in the front with me as they can often be quite fun when you try to get a conversation going. The hard of hearing ones can entertain for hours along the lines of "How long have you lived in Bexhill"? The reply is often something like "I know, I hope it doesn't rain." My passenger today was fine, however, and I explained that we were going to have a bit of a ride around and that although we might look lost at times, I hoped that wouldn't be the case.

The lady in the back had the best chat up line I've heard in my entire life and she is welcome in my car anytime. Three minutes after setting off in my 18 year old Bentley she asked, "What a beautiful car, is it brand new?"

Every trip like this has what I call 'the point of no return,' and you are now committed to arriving at your destination. We had passed our point of no return with no more left or right turns to be had when I received a request from the back seat.

"We've left our camera at home, is there any chance we could pop back and get it?"

I agreed to the request but pointed out that we had no option but to drive straight past the hotel. As we turned the corner and the hotel came into view, there he was with his video camera, thinking to himself, 'Good, here they come and then, there they go.' His face must have been an absolute picture. I could see him videoing me once again disappearing into the distance. I tried to control my laughter but felt my shoulders going up and down and that was a dead giveaway to my passengers in the back so I had to say something in explanation,

"I'm afraid that rather appeals to my sense of humour and I feel sure that will be the best bit of your video."

Fantastic.

I didn't have to tell him where to shove his video camera or to suggest he cover it in Vaseline first.

MAD WORLD 57
THE BROTHEL

This is only a short one but it made me laugh which hurts like hell at the moment. Please don't make me laugh.

After being knocked off yet another motorcycle recently which resulted in a trip to the hospital on a spinal board in the back of an ambulance, I received some nice emails to cheer me up and then Jayne rang me during her half hour lunch break on Friday to see how I was doing.

"Jayne," I said, "you must get some copies of the other *Observer* as there is a picture of me in it with the ladies from the WI." I had received an email which had been sent to me with a picture attached.

"Ok," she replied, "But guess what? I've been reading our *Observer* while I was eating my sandwiches and did you know there is a brothel in our town?"

"Oh I don't think I'm up to that at the moment." I replied.

I mistakenly thought she was going to treat me to try and cheer me up.

MAD WORLD 58
CHRISTMAS 2007

Christmas 2007. What is going on out there?

Two Saturdays before Christmas, I decided to do my Christmas shopping after work. On the way to my car, I saw two male Special Constables hassling the young lady who sells the *Big Issue*. They emptied her pockets and moved her on her way. What was that all about?

On the same afternoon, we were shopping in our town centre and I watched as 3 young musicians set up to play Christmas carols to the shoppers. They set up on a street corner and were the smartest turned out teenagers I've seen in a very long time. Five minutes later, we observed the same small group being made to pack up and move on by a female Special Constable.

I'm told the Christmas cards we're sending this year are less likely to say Happy Christmas as they may offend. Apparently, it is more correct to say, 'Seasons Greetings.'

Moving on. The Highlights.

I don't usually get involved with the discussions at work relating to Christmas tips as it is a private thing. But the one story I did relay to my colleagues went down well. I mentioned that as I was delivering past the local pub one day, a customer of mine came running out and along the road towards me waving a twenty pound note in the air. Upon reaching my van he said, "Steve, can you change this?" to which I asked in a disgruntled voice, "Well, how much do you want back?" "I'll go halves with you," the customer replied.

After giving him a tenner back he disappeared back into the pub to buy another drink.

One of my colleagues found this a little more amusing than most and I enquired as to why.

"Steve," he said, "surely you aren't telling us you can spot a twenty pound note from a hundred yards?"

I've been doing the job a long time!

I went to the village lunch for the old folks in the village hall, as I do every Christmas.

The oldest chap in the village was unable to attend this year which was a shame as he is nearly 94. However, his name did crop up in conversation. Apparently he doesn't consider himself to be a local. He didn't move to the village until he was 2 years old. He had previously lived in the next village, about 2 miles away. To be a local, your parents and grandparents have to have been born in the village, so they say. Blimey.

Due to the later start times imposed on me by my employer, I spent the week leading up to Christmas arriving at my last call at anything up to 4pm. One afternoon I delivered to an elderly lady at 3pm. As I walked in she said: "Stephen, I've been waiting for a man." Why are they always over 80 when they say that? She was sitting at the kitchen table waiting to make her mince pies. She had all the pastry cases lined up in the tin and an enormous jar of mincemeat stood beside the tin but she couldn't undo the lid.

What a good job I have so many calls on my round where I just let myself in. What a good job I don't just do deliveries.

And last of all: An ex-manager of Jayne's who took redundancy earlier this year with £42,000, wrote in Jayne's Christmas card: 'I wish you, health, happiness and redundancy.' Jayne dreams of that!

MAD WORLD 59
HAVE SOME VOUCHERS

I know I haven't had a good word to say about my employer for a few years now. Something that happened yesterday did nothing to improve matters. I felt the need this morning to contact a company by email for their advice. It was only when I considered sharing my experience with you, my friends, that it suddenly made me laugh out loud. My employer strikes again.
I don't hold out much hope for my gold watch.

Hello - Love 2 Shop,
That's exactly what I tried to do yesterday with £80 of Love2Shop vouchers which had been sent to me within the past year in recognition of my 20 years of service with my employer. Of course, it was no great surprise that no one would accept them as that is the sort of thing I've come to expect from my employer. However, I was wondering if you could advise me on my next move before I contact my employer and tell them where to stick their vouchers.
The numbers of the vouchers that I have in £10.00 denominations are:
05161108752600, 700, 800, 900
05161108753000, 100, 200, 300

It was my birthday this week and we thought we'd have a day out in Brighton and do some shopping. We aren't really very good shoppers but thought we'd make the effort. After discovering that Virgin were no longer Virgin, we were pleased that they were prepared to accept Love2Shop vouchers except for the ones I had in my hand. I have no idea what has happened so please could you help me?

My employee number is: My home address is: Home phone number:

Please could you take the time and trouble to help me as it would be very much appreciated.

You cannot imagine the disappointment and embarrassment we felt.

Regards,
Steve.

MAD WORLD 60
THE COUNTER STAFF ARE GETTING BIGGER

OK, this one's for Jayne as it is she who has to work there, but you might enjoy it if I share it with you. Oh dear, I've just read this Mad World after writing it and it is particularly bad. Sorry. Maybe I shouldn't write when I've got such a bad head. I will probably get shot at dawn for this one.

As you may remember from my previous ramblings, since this wonderful Government of ours relieved the burden from our Post Offices of selling television licences and paying out so many pensions and benefits, they have been set free to panic and strive to find alternative sources of income. This has enabled the incomes of many sub-post offices to dive and consequently face closure while the main offices continue to get ever more desperate to sell you more than the stamps you went in to buy. You may recall the techniques used by the counter clerks last year where they would just pounce on every customer, regardless of age, colour or religion and ask them if they would like a quote for car insurance? If the customer didn't have a car of their own, they were then offered the chance to take out a Post Office home phone so they could phone someone for a lift. Things have moved on since then. Those same counter clerks are now highly trained and sit there like coiled springs ready to leap into action using their well-rehearsed opening lines. They are trained to spot the link between one product and another. We aren't just talking small fry here such as when a little old lady asks for

6 stamps and gets offered the chance to buy 6 envelopes to stick them on. If someone goes in to buy euros they get offered travel insurance. If someone goes to pay by cheque they get offered the chance to take out a Post Office credit card. Yes, why pay now when you can just incur some more debt? They even do broadband where you are guaranteed to stay offline. A girl I work with took that out and she spends so much time chatting to the chap on the helpline that it can only be a matter of time before they start dating.

The counter clerks are given incentives and rewards to help them to perform.

One incentive is, if you perform badly, you will then have the privilege of a Manager sitting behind you for a day listening to your selling technique. Or rather your lack thereof. Rewards usually come in the form of sweets and other edible treats. Yes, it's just like being back at school. If you go into any main Post Office these days, it's easy to spot the best sellers amongst the counter clerks as they definitely aren't the skinny ones. The company even came up with a scheme where the Best Performing Office would get an all-expenses paid weekend away. Unfortunately, the sales graph went straight through the floor when it dawned on the staff that the all-expenses paid weekend away was to be taken together with their colleagues. You won't believe this next bit but I'm telling you, it's true. In our local main office, the back room staff consists of a couple of real Teletubbies. They seemed to be missing out on the treats so they devised a dastardly plan. Counter clerks now get the customer interested in a product and then hand the customer over to one of the back room staff who go on to complete the deal by showing the customer where to sign. No doubt both counter clerk and back room staff then get a sweetie each. With 10 counter clerks and only 2 back room staff no wonder the back room staff are in desperate need of a clothing allowance.

The point of all this? Now you know the background, you might enjoy the following tale. Following a transaction yesterday which was made by a gentleman customer, he whipped out his cheque book to pay. The conversation went like this:

Counter Clerk: "Do you have a credit card, Sir?"

Customer: "No."

Counter Clerk: "Would you be interested in taking out one of our credit cards?"

Customer: "Yes, I would."

Counter Clerk: "Right, I just have to ask you a few questions to see if you qualify to apply and then, if you are still interested, I'll hand you over to one of my colleagues who will help you to fill out the form and show you where to sign."

The Counter Clerk then proceeded to ask the usual questions like: Do you have a UK bank or building society account? The Customer answered all the questions and said that he was still really interested in signing up for a Post Office credit card. The counter clerk asked him to wait for just a moment while she went to get one of the Teletubbies to haul themselves out of their chair and waddle out the front to complete the deal. The conversation hadn't quite finished though:

Customer: "Before you go, can I just ask you one more question, please?"

Counter Clerk: "Certainly, what's your question?"

Customer: "What's a Credit Card?"

MAD WORLD 61
TYRE KICKER

Here we go again with a bit of employer bashing but in fairness, it's their own fault. I have a colleague who started suffering from epileptic fits/seizures. Jayne knows from personal experience with her Dad how frightening that can be. As a result, my colleague was off work for quite a while before being encouraged back to work on light duties. He gets to sit in the caller's office on a stool listening to music through his earpieces. He's banned from driving while the doctors get his medication right and in the hope that it will remain right for a long time to come. About a year or more, I believe. He gets to work and home again by bus or is given a lift by the management. He has since had one collapse at work and was taken away by Ambulance but they enticed him back to work again on the strict understanding that he wouldn't be left alone in the office.

On Monday of this week, it couldn't be guaranteed that someone else would be in the office with him all day. So, was he told to stay at home? Not on your Nelly. He was sent out on a walking delivery, which he had never done before on his own. Thankfully, he survived that ordeal but it could have so easily ended badly.

Then we got to Wednesday. Looking forward to the weekend already.

It was 5.30 pm and Jayne was starting to prepare our evening meal, dinner for the two of us, when the phone rang. "Hello Steve." It was a female neighbour. "I need your help with something and I was wondering if you could, at your convenience, help me check the tyre pressures on my car." This neighbour is a fantastic neighbour and has done brilliantly well to carry on living down here since her husband died a few years ago. Her children live in London and she really doesn't want to move back there. So we do all we can for her when she needs our help or advice on things. She doesn't bother us very often and is always willing to let me use her drive or garage if I need to. I half missed what she said next as I was just working out if I had time to do her tyre pressures there and then as she was planning to use her car the following day. Then she said: "I've kicked the tyres but I'm still not sure if they're OK."

"How about now?" I suggested, "Bring your handbook out with you so we can see what the tyre pressures should be."

About 2 minutes later we were on her drive. I had my tyre pressure gauge and foot pump from my garage and our neighbour was looking in her handbook for the tyre pressures. I double checked she was looking at the right page. No, I'm not joking. The lesson began: "Now, I usually look at my tyres first and if they look OK, then they usually are."

"But the front ones look a bit flat compared with the back ones." she said.

I continued, "With modern tyres they will look a bit podgy on the front as that is where all the weight of the engine is and that's how they tend to look. It's normal. Look at the front tyres on your car and then come across and look at the front tyres on my car and you'll see what I mean."

So she went up to one of her front tyres and gave it a kick that Beckham would have been proud of. 'What the Hell?' I thought, I can't believe my eyes. Then she was heading towards my Volvo where I was now standing. "Stop right there," I almost shouted, "Why have you just booted one of your tyres?" She replied: "Because that's what my husband used to do."

When you live on our road it is always interesting to see who will be next to finish up in the care home. I hadn't realised we were in a race.

MAD WORLD 62
PREMIUM BONDS

All my life I've admired people from my parents and grandparents generations for their level of resilience and toughness which undoubtedly comes from the experiences they endured during and just after the war years. I hope I never have to experience the hardships that they did as I feel I would fall short in the fortitude department. However, I sometimes question their priorities.

A very elderly gentleman staggered up to the counter in our local main Post Office and asked the clerk, "Please could I have a form for cashing in Premium Bonds?"

As the clerk turned to go and get a copy of the appropriate form the elderly gentleman added, "For someone who is dead."

A few moments later the clerk returned, and proceeded to pass the form through to the elderly gentleman who, as he was preparing to go on his way, said,

"She isn't actually dead yet, but I've been told she won't last the week."

MAD WORLD 63
NEW VAN

I recently received a letter from my employer telling me that they have now decided they can't afford for me to retire at the previously agreed age of 60. I think I might be giving them a surprise on that one when the time comes. Two days after I received the letter, I was told that a brand new van was awaiting me if I would care to drive to our workshop to collect it. Maybe you can't see any connection there, so I'll carry on.

Our company vehicles get replaced every 3 to 4 years as a matter of course. This cuts down on the expense of MOT work. It also means that the majority of the company vehicles still retain some kind of resale value when they're put in to an auction. My vans, when I've finished with them, usually go for scrap.

My old Peugeot van was a good van until a head-on collision in one of the country lanes resulted in it being almost as wide as it was long. The accident wasn't my fault as I had managed to stop but my 'opponent' hadn't. The replacement was a Vauxhall Combi van of dubious quality which has now come to the end of its life at 39,000 miles. So, it was with great excitement that I set off to Tonbridge to collect my new van. Naturally, as expected, my nice new van is an extremely similar shade of red to my old van but it doesn't have the go faster yellow stripe along each side. I noticed at once the cost saving exercise that had taken place with the dust caps for the axle covers. There weren't any. The axle ends were already a nice rusty red colour despite the milometer only showing 11 miles on the clock when I picked it up.

Picture the scene if you can. There I was, driving my nice new van on the 40 minute run back to the office from the workshop. As I said before, the milometer was only showing 11 miles when I collected the van and, despite my disappointment that it was yet another top quality product [I don't think so] from Vauxhall, I was trying to look on the bright side. The suspension worked and wasn't knackered like my old van and the bodywork had a complete covering of paint. My old van hadn't been washed for a year due to the fact that I had borrowed a pressure washer on one of the farms to wash my van down and it stripped some of the paint off. So I left it covered in mud after that. My new van has a side door which I've never had before. I'm looking forward to using that once I remember it's there. And providing it works, of course.

'Things could be worse' I thought, at least it wasn't a fold up Ford.

Then my optimism took a huge knock.

In the space of just a few miles I saw two Vauxhall Combi vans like mine.

One was on the back of a low loader recovery truck and the other was being towed by the AA.

MAD WORLD 64
BETTER THAN A LOTTERY TICKET

Pets. We all love our pets whether they be cats, dogs, hammy hamsters or guinea pigs.

We have Oliver our cat and we haven't experienced living with a dog since moving away from our parents. It's interesting to see and hear what goes on in other households though.

On one occasion when we had afternoon tea with some friends of ours, I watched in amazement as the pet dog helped himself to the biggest piece of cake on the table while no one else was looking. He managed a far bigger slice than I ever could. I brushed the whole episode aside as being nothing more than a hierarchy thing from the dog's point of view. He got first pick while I, being no more than a mere visitor, had to wait my turn which was much further down the pecking order. I didn't think anything would match that episode but a story I was told by a colleague at work came pretty close.

Since my employer decided to take a leap forward from Victorian times and had introduced meal breaks about 6 months ago, I've enjoyed having a morning meal break with a colleague I've known for many years. My friend has several cats and dogs who, collectively it would seem, eat a similar amount of food to what our Oliver manages on his own. That could explain why Oliver's BMI [Body Mass Index] isn't much better than mine.

One morning, as I was tucking into my marmalade sandwiches, I got into a discussion with my friend about our pets and the conversation soon got onto the subject of what goes in and what comes out. I was somewhat wary of the subject as I didn't consider it to be a particularly nice topic for mealtimes but I stuck with it. Apparently my friend's dogs don't stop to chew their food if they're eating something they shouldn't. Our Oliver doesn't have a choice since the vet took out nearly all his teeth. He swallows everything whole. My friend then went on to tell me of an unfortunate incident that occurred when one of her dogs was a puppy. The puppy got hold of an envelope that contained money and ate the lot. Thank goodness he didn't chew it.

My friend spent the next few days wearing rubber gloves each time she walked the puppy and gradually got herself a complete refund. She then washed the notes and took them to the bank to exchange them, telling the cashier she had accidentally put some money through the washing machine.

The story itself struck me as funny but I couldn't help picturing other members of the public as they watched this puppy going along and stopping every so often to deposit a few more fivers or ten pound notes onto the grass verge or the pavement. The supply and demand for puppies at the local breeders must have been amazing as all the locals decided that a puppy was a better bet than a lottery ticket.

MAD WORLD 65
WINDY ON THE COAST

Here we go again. Didn't think I could possibly have anything to say this week, what with being on holiday and all that. But how about this for starters?

Monday, 10th March. The worst storms of the winter hit the UK. People living on the coast were advised to stay indoors. People living further inland were advised to stay there. Don't go near the coast, were the words of warning. We got off lightly compared with some parts of the country, with just 70-80mph winds and torrential rain. With the forecast as it was, we postponed taking the Rolls to Goudhurst for its annual service and MOT until Tuesday. No problem there then. Stay indoors.

Guess which day of the year our new greenhouse was erected in our back garden?

You had to see it to believe it.

On Monday afternoon, Jayne went into the building society to get a cheque to pay for a family present for her parents' upcoming golden wedding anniversary. As she waited, dripping water onto the counter and forming a puddle on the floor with the rain hitting the shop window driven by 80mph winds, the cashier commented on the weather.

Jayne told her: "We had a new greenhouse erected this morning."

The counter clerk inserted Jayne's building society book into the cheque making machine and the cheque got printed straight across two pages of the open book by mistake.

I don't know why these situations amuse me so much. I can only put it down to being tipped out of the pram by one of my brothers when I was a baby and hitting my head on the concrete. Must have affected the part of my brain that was expected, in later life, to give me some level of intelligence. I hope some of my tales still amuse some of you and, if so, did you also get tipped out of your pram?

MAD WORLD 66
CLOSING POST OFFICES

We continue to see the double standards we expect these days from our politicians. For example, voting on the continued closure of Post Offices up and down the country and then standing outside their own local Post Office on a Saturday morning actively campaigning to keep it open. The closure programme is a done and dusted affair regardless of how many of the public, celebrities or two faced politicians try to stop a particular branch or sub-post office from closing. Anyone who believes a save our Post Office campaign will work would also believe, presumably, that my employer was only pulling my leg when they said I would have to work 5 more years to get my pension.

So, Post Office Counters know which subs are closing and you would assume it would make good business sense to recruit a few more staff to coincide with a nearby closure. But, Post Office Counters don't believe in good business sense. Consequently, it works like this.

The nearby sub-post office is due to shut, so, at the same time, Post Office Counters begin recruiting. The sub-post office shuts and its customers give the main Post Office a try. The main Post Office has about 10 windows for counter clerks to serve from but only has 2 windows open at peak times. The queues in the main Post Office go around the office several times and out the door into the street. Four to six weeks go by like this until the new customers get disillusioned and find other ways of buying half a dozen stamps. New recruits are now trained to a standard where they can inflict real stress on their customers and are put into place ready to serve the long queues which are no longer there. New recruits cotton on as to why they were only given a 3 month contract.

The elderly population is used to seeing this process repeated over and over again. They've survived the Blitz, Hitler and the inconvenience of rationing and they are more than a match for the sheer incompetence of the Post Office management. The old folk fall into two categories when waiting in the queue in our main local Post Office. There are those who have already had new hips and knees fitted and they stand quietly waiting their turn. The others are still on the NHS waiting list for adjustments, modifications, and replacements. With the queues going out the door and the prospect of a 20-30 minute wait before reaching the counter, they come well equipped. Several have been spotted with the new Zimmer, complete with a seat. With the Post Office closure programme designed to give us all access to a Post Office within 3 miles, I can fully understand why your pension goes up by 25 pence when you reach the age of 80. It is incentive money. Incentive to polish the Zimmer, oil the wheels and give it a go as you try to get your pension.

But my favourite tale, and the foundation stone of this Mad World was that of one particular elderly lady who really couldn't see the need to waste time in the anticipated lengthy queue. Like everyone else, she needed her half a dozen stamps and knew the local main Post Office was going through the usual exercise of trying to lose a few more customers so it was likely to be a long wait to get served at the counter. She joined the back of the queue and once she'd managed to get inside the Post Office, she pulled out her wool and knitting needles and started knitting. I dread to think how big the jumper was by the time she reached the counter.

MAD WORLD 67
CLOCKS

Sorry I haven't had anything to write lately but from my point of view that's quite good news as it means I've been having a quiet life for a change.

There was an interesting situation at work though when I returned from my deliveries on Friday. My mate, the PHG, pointed out that I was going to be on holiday for this coming week according to the duty sheet. I simply told him that I was most definitely not on holiday and if they chose to give me the week off, I wouldn't bother coming back.

"In that case then," said the PHG, "can you work your day off on Monday?"

In the space of less than 5 minutes I had gone from being on holiday for a week to working a 6 day week.

As you all know, since Jayne inherited a grandfather clock, my interest in clocks of all sizes has really taken off. This time last year we had 2 clocks in the bungalow excluding anything electrically or battery operated. Basically, any empty horizontal space such as the sideboard, shelves and wall unit tops appear to look much better when filled with clocks. We now have 20. As a friend of ours said to Jayne today, "The future looks bleak." Brilliant.

Jayne mentioned to a friend of ours who has a clock shop that she would like to attend an antiques fair one day. So he very kindly sent us some tickets.

Today we visited our very first antiques fair which was held at Sandown Park. Our friend from the clock shop had a stand there and, fortunately, from my point of view, he had decided to have the day off and his lovely wife was manning the stand. There was a good variety of stands displaying antiques of all kinds. One memorable conversation Jayne and I had whilst viewing the items on display, was when Jayne was admiring a tavern table from 1770-1800. When I commented to Jayne that the price of the table was £14,700, she asked me if that included the chairs? "No." I replied, "They're £7,700 extra." It would be such a shame to buy the tavern table and not be able to afford the chairs. So we walked away.

We enjoyed the day and used the event to collect a quarter chiming mantle clock of mine which had been overhauled by my friend at his clock shop. It is most definitely not an antique clock and is, in fact, one of the least attractive clocks in my very small collection. But it does sound lovely when it chimes. Due to the low value of my clock and the cheap appearance of the case, I went prepared with a Marks and Spencer carrier bag in which to hide it as I carried it out of the building. It didn't fit entirely inside the bag and one end of the clock was left protruding slightly from the open end as I carried it, right way up, under my arm. Maybe I don't look like the type to be visiting antiques fairs. I don't know. I had left my woolly hat in the car. Maybe I simply look like a crook. I followed Jayne towards the exit door and, as she went to open the door, I was suddenly accosted by security. The little security man insisted I produce a green or was it brown card to provide proof that what I was carrying under my arm was in fact paid for. I was completely unable to do as he requested and tried to convince him that the item under my arm was in fact mine. I had simply collected it from an exhibitor at the fair. Of course, by now, people were beginning to watch as this undoubted hooligan was brought to book. Then the situation, from my point of view, became unbearably embarrassing as Jayne came to the rescue.

Jayne started to take my cheap looking mantle clock out of the bag revealing it for all to see and saying, "It's not even an antique, look."

As the security man returned to his post, laughing uncontrollably, I kid you not, I told him, "If it was something I had bought here today I would have carried it through here proudly for all to see."

Jayne's thinking of taking us to an auction next. Can't wait. Maybe I'll fit in better there.

MAD WORLD 68
WHAT GOES UP MUST COME DOWN

Here we go again. After a disappointing 2 weeks of annual leave, apart from a brilliant day at the clock shop last Saturday, Jayne has asked me to write something up. It isn't a subject I would ever go near with a barge pole usually but, as it was Jayne's request and with me having to return to the grotty job of working tomorrow, I had better have a go at writing while I still have a sense of humour left.

Earlier this year it was Jayne's parents' 50th wedding anniversary. They are both in their early seventies. A big party was held as they are great party people and amongst all the gifts that they received, there was a special gift from the family. A speech was performed on the night by Jayne's elder brother who announced that, following consultation with Jayne's friend who used to be a photographer and is now an undertaker, a special gift had been organised via the local coroner. An envelope was presented to Jayne's parents who thought some sort of funeral package had been organised. However, the surprise gift was in fact a hot air balloon ride. The local coroner has a hot air balloon and a suitable date was arranged for Jayne's parents to take to the skies. Following the cancellation of the original date due to bad weather which is no surprise with the summer we have had, several more dates were arranged and then cancelled again at the last minute. Until yesterday. Then it was on.

It was our job to deliver Jayne's parents to the departure point at Bodiam Castle and a small crowd of family and friends assembled to watch 3 hot air balloons take off simultaneously, one of which was carrying Jayne's parents. All the usual comments were made such as 'have you made your will?', and my comment of, 'if the balloon runs on hot air then with Jayne's Mum aboard, it should go like a rocket.' We watched the 3 hot air balloons float majestically out of sight and, having arranged for Jayne's uncle to sit in the pub and await their return, we came home. We were so relieved that the balloon flight had taken place at long last. We were home about 6.30 pm. At around 8 pm the phone rang. It would appear that Jayne's Mum must have stopped talking at some point during the flight, a record in itself, and she was now on the phone to us.

"Hello Steve, we crash landed and we are now in casualty at the Conquest Hospital." She went on to tell me that Jayne's Dad was waiting for some stitches. He was waiting for stitches and yet here I was, in stitches myself. Don't you just love it when a plan comes together?

I think for their 60th Wedding Anniversary we should stick to something safer and just sign them up for a bungee jump.

MAD WORLD 69
HOW MANY DINNERS IN A DAY?

For those of you who enjoy the Mad World series, sorry it's been so long since I last had something worth writing about. For those of you who endure the Mad World series, tough, Big Steve is going to tell you anyway.

Remember, I deliver to a very rural village where I rarely knock on doors but just walk in, dump the mail and walk out again and I'm not embarrassed to admit to knowing the location of one or two well stocked cake tins. Fortunately for me, I rarely have brain waves. However, I had one today and it proved rather spectacularly to be my undoing. I take two lots of sandwiches to work each day, one lot for breakfast and the other for lunch. I can't wait until I get home to have my lunch as I never know what time I'll actually get home. I usually complete my delivery and then open my sandwiches to eat on the way back to the office. But now it's December, I'm getting later and later making the return trip to the office. In an effort to control my headaches, I had the brain wave today that maybe I should stop while on my deliveries and have something to eat. That is often what I have to do in December. So, for the first time this year I stopped the van at 12.20 pm and ate my lunch. At 12.30 pm I was on my way again. How I wish I had crystal balls as I was totally unprepared for what happened next.

At 12.50 pm, after observing an unusual car in the drive, I walked into a house where an elderly lady lives, bowled in to the kitchen as usual and she had two elderly lady friends sitting with her at the table.

"Good, Stephen we've been waiting for you to come because we've got your lunch in the oven. Sit yourself down and we can start. It's fish and chips," said the lady of the house.

"But I'm a bit late," I replied.

"Never mind that," says one of the visitors, "You'll just have to say you were held up in traffic."

Traffic? In this village?

I pointed out that my credibility in the office would be much higher if I were to tell the truth and say I had been accosted by three lovely ladies. Nevertheless, I took off my woolly hat and coat and sat down as instructed. Out of the Aga came four neatly wrapped bundles from the chip shop and I watched as they were emptied, plonk, plonk, plonk, plonk on to the plates. Guess which one was selected for the hungry postman? The three ladies were too polite to mention my eyes being out on stalks as I gazed down on the largest fish that could ever have swum in the sea. They made sure that my plate was surrounded by salt, vinegar, tartare sauce, brown sauce and tomato sauce. Sadly, I don't really like fish. I'm more of a sausage and chips sort of chap. But I did give it my absolute best shot. As I spread the surplus batter around the plate, one of the visiting ladies announced: "I've made an apple pie for pudding." 'Oh, yippee.' I thought to myself. Out of the Aga comes this huge homemade apple pie. It got cut 4 ways. Guess who got the largest slice? A big pot of cream was passed over to me so that I could tuck in as no doubt I would be wanting to be on my way fairly shortly. Such kindness from these lovely ladies. Such a bellyache for me. I staggered to my feet, collecting my hat and coat as I made my way to the kitchen door and thanked the three ladies very much and couldn't stop myself from asking, "Will you all be coming again next year?"

MAD WORLD 70
CHRISTMAS 2008

I thought it might be nice to do a Mad World Christmas Highlights 2008.

That should make it the shortest Mad World of all time then.

But first of all, I'm going to share a few observations that I made following my recent trip to Hospital after collapsing at the doctor's.

1. If you collapse while waiting in the waiting room of your doctor's surgery, you get to see the doctor much faster than if you just wait your turn. In fact, he comes to you, rather than you going to him.

2. Paramedics have a trick way of getting blood out of your finger after 4 failed attempts. They pump, pump, pump, pump on the blood pressure monitor that is wrapped around your arm and, hey presto, blood spurts out of your finger. Magic.

3. I've tried this several times now and it definitely works.

If you arrive at the Hospital by Ambulance, you get seen by the doctors much quicker than if you just walk in the front door.

4. Every doctor who has a look at you in the Hospital asks if you have been eating and drinking normally. But you can lie there on the bench for anything up to 6 hours, including lunch time, and nobody offers you anything to eat or drink. If they think you look thirsty, they just pump fluid straight in to your arm.

5. That oxygen is damned good stuff. I would love to have a bottle of that at home to clear my head from time to time.

Christmas Highlight from 2008?

A couple of weeks before Christmas, and before I became so ill during the Festive Season, I answered a knock at the door. It was the Betterware man who had come to deliver our small order. Jayne had ordered 2 kiddies' toys to give to the nieces or nephews for Christmas.

I handed the money to the Betterware man and he handed me the carrier bag containing the 2 kiddies' toys. I was totally unprepared for what the Betterware man then said. Needless to say I won't tell you what my reply to him was as it was a comment that was undoubtedly unfit for these pages. Suffice to say that my beard is obviously an awful lot greyer than I had realised.

The Betterware man said: "Presents for the grandchildren, Sir?"

Happy New Year to all my Mad World readers. Let's hope 2009 isn't as bleak as predicted.

MAD WORLD 71
ALL THE GADGETS

I'm not particularly into all the latest technology and gadgets and quite recently even had my mobile phone disconnected by my service provider. I only have the mobile for emergencies and vital calls. But when attempting a vital call to Jayne recently to tell her it might be a good time to start cooking my dinner as I'd be home in half an hour, I discovered my mobile phone was no longer working. I was sure I had plenty of credit as I have a pay as you go type contract. So, I rang the mobile phone company using our landline and I was told I had not abided by the terms of the contract and my phone had been disconnected 2 weeks previously. The very kind chap on the other end of the phone explained that he could reconnect my phone but I really should try to use it at least once every 6 months. I apologised for my mistake, thanked him for reconnecting me and told him I would make a note on the calendar to remind me to phone someone using my mobile in September.

My lack of interest in all mod cons means our television in the lounge is so old it has no scart socket (whatever a scart socket is?) so the first 3 DVD players that Jayne won in competitions had to be sold. I see no need for things such as dishwashers, new kitchens and new bathrooms. The money can be far better spent on cars, bikes and longcase clocks. I did make one concession when the television in the kitchen went pop. I could see it was necessary to provide Jayne with a new one so that she has something to watch whilst cooking my dinner, washing up or ironing my shirts.

However, I do have a friend who has every labour saving device that is known to man. His daily car has a coating on the paintwork that repels dirt and the boot opens and closes at the touch of a button on his remote control. He doesn't even have to lean on the boot to close it. Brilliant to watch. Indoors he has the requisite dishwasher and even a robotic vacuum cleaner. The vacuum cleaner, which has a rechargeable battery, is similar in size to a pair of bathroom scales. Once it is switched on, it happily goes all around the bungalow hoovering the carpets by crisscrossing the rooms, turning around each time it reaches the skirting board.

This particular friend usually phones me each week for a chat. He phones me because, so he says, he can afford the phone bill. That's the right kind of friend to have. Last night, the phone rang at the usual time but it was my friend's wife on the line. She told me my friend couldn't speak to me this week as he had put his back out. Following a fairly lengthy story about how marvellous NHS direct had been and all the advice they had given, I just had to enquire: "How did he put his back out?"

The lady on the line said: "Well, as you know we have a robotic vacuum cleaner."

"Yes," I replied, "don't tell me he fell over it?"

"No," She said, "he put his back out when he bent down to switch it on."

MAD WORLD 72
YOU OLD TART

What a year it's been. Haven't had the right mind set for writing for 7 months but at long last something has happened that really appealed to my sense of humour. All my life I've been simply brilliant at opening my mouth and putting my foot right in it. Jump straight in with both feet usually. But now I appear to have mastered the art of getting into trouble without even opening my mouth.

In my daily job, I drive a Vauxhall Combi van which is just a fraction too tall for people to see over the top of. The alleyway we drive through to get from the office yard and out on to the street is so narrow that you have to fold one wing mirror in so as to get the van through the alleyway without scraping the walls. The last bit of the alleyway is a tunnel as the property is built across the top of it. We emerge from the tunnel, cross the pedestrian pavement, drive a further two vehicle lengths to cross a side road and then we get on to the high street.

It was 9.15 am on a Friday morning two weeks before Christmas Day so there was a lot to do. Everyone was under pressure to get out the door and on to their deliveries. In my case, I shan't return to the office for 5 to 6 hours as I have 40 miles to cover. As I emerged from the tunnel, I waited to cross the pedestrian pavement with the rear of my van still blocking the tunnel. In front of me were two more vans waiting to be let out into what was left of the rush hour traffic. One of the new recruits started to bounce his mail trolley off of the back of my van. Bang, bang, bang, as everything is amplified in the rear of a van. I decided to stick my van in to reverse and show him that my van's weight will soon outdo his ice cream trolley. At the same time, I decided to put my foot down on the accelerator so as to give him some diesel fumes to chew on while he was waiting. A little old lady appeared to the left on the pavement in front of me and I gestured to her, by waving my hand, to indicate that it was safe for her to walk across in front of my van. After all, I was going nowhere due to the two vans still waiting ahead of me. Bearing in mind everything that I've told you up to now, the little old lady couldn't see over my van and neither can anyone standing behind my van see the little old lady. And the inside of these vans amplify any noise.

Another colleague of mine who had appeared on the scene, opened the back door of my van and bellowed at the top of his voice to me, "Come on, move it you old tart," and shut the door again. The two vans in front of me were suddenly let out into the traffic, the little old lady was now past my van and I saw my chance and took off.

Many hours later, I returned to the office to hear that I was in big trouble as a little old lady had come into the office that morning, just after I had left, and complained about the chap with the ginger beard who had called her an old tart.

Didn't she wonder how I managed it without moving my lips?

MAD WORLD 73
SAY A PRAYER

Well, here we go again. Something happened that amused me and I thought I'd share it with you. As you know, I'm not particularly religious but I don't have a problem with those who are. I do, however, marvel occasionally at the strength of their faith.

It was Saturday 30th January and the temperature outside was -3C as I scraped the frost from the windows of my Volvo at 5 am. In fact, this is a perfect example as to why, at this time of year, my woolly hat only gets removed occasionally at night and the scarf that is growing nicely out of my chin remains in place until April. However, the frost and ice I then encountered whilst out on delivery was a lot easier to deal with than the generous snow fall I've had to tackle in recent weeks. 40 miles of country lanes and farm tracks is always a challenge in those conditions on the days that I'm actually allowed out in my van. All was well until I delivered to the large Christian Centre that's on my round. It's about half a mile down a private single carriageway, a tarmac drive with the occasional passing bay. The drive itself was in perfect condition for traffic but, with it being Saturday morning, I had to tackle a constant flow of vehicles coming towards me as they headed for the gate. Saturday morning is often going home time for those who have been on their knees all week on a residential course or retreat. The cars coming towards me had a variety of differing standards of frost clearance on their windscreens. As you have all no doubt witnessed in your time, some people clear their windows properly and others just scrape a small hole to peer through. After taking avoiding action several times, I suddenly had to pull my van right onto the grass. Coming towards me was a car with none of the frost cleared from the windscreen at all. I couldn't believe my eyes. This surely had to be the Wally of the winter so far. Either that or he had the most remarkable Sat Nav yet to come on the market. I sat and watched as the car passed by at about 2 mph. I could see the driver quite clearly as no frost had formed on the side windows on the offside.

The driver was wearing a nice, crisp, white dog collar. Faith indeed.

It reminded me of a tale told to me on several occasions by a couple of elderly friends of mine who, for many years, ran a taxi service in the village. Both gentlemen are in their nineties now but have remained good friends. They drove all manner of village folk to all manner of appointments, events, airports and so on. One regular customer of theirs was a local clergyman who resided for many years at the large Christian Centre. Each trip up the drive from the house included a request to my taxi driving friends to pull over in to one of the passing places whereupon the clergyman then prayed, out loud, for the good Lord to watch over a safe journey to his destination.

If any clever Dick ever tries that one on me when travelling in one of my cars, I shall be politely suggesting that they might prefer to get out and walk.

MAD WORLD 74
HOLIDAY COVER

It's February 14th. So what? But it's Valentine's Day. Oh dear. Never mind, there's always next year I suppose.

My van seems to have taken a liking to spending nights in the village. Last week it had a night in the village when a spring broke in a rear brake drum and the brake shoes jammed on. Yesterday, after already having to change a puncture, I then broke down again when I lost the gears. So, my van is in the village for the whole weekend this time. And back at the office? Well.

In our small office we have 2 employees who don't usually go out on deliveries. One is the manager and one is what used to be called a PHG. It is his job to man the small office that contains all the important stuff like van keys, log books, special delivery items and the safe.

The manager that we've had for the past 12 months is affectionately known as The Grim Reaper as he has saved the company hundreds of pounds by costing us the same in reduced overtime. As I understand it, Five Bellies is still our proper manager although he hasn't been seen for the past year. The PHG has his annual leave next week so his job needs to be covered. There is a chap who usually stands in for the PHG but he has had trouser worm trouble and is now unavailable. For over 20 years of my doing the job, I have never known a colleague who had the energy to actually start a family while employed at our place of work. If you don't have kids when you start on this job, you can forget it. You simply won't have the energy for that sort of thing. At least that's my experience anyway. Either that or it could just be something they put in the tea. However, we now have an entrant for the Guinness Book of Records as one of my colleagues has not only become a dad this week but he managed the feat with one of the female workers in our office. Apparently, current regulations entitle new fathers to have 2 weeks off work to celebrate the new arrival. Unfortunately, the reality is that he will now spend the next 18 years paying for the little blighter.

The Grim Reaper is a bit sharper than Five Bellies was and had the birth date marked in his diary. The Grim Reaper had made arrangements for another member of staff to spend all of this past week being trained on the PHG job so that we have cover for him when he's on holiday next week. Brilliant bit of forward thinking, don't you think? We aren't used to having managers that are that bright. The trainee has been working alongside the PHG learning the job, making notes of what goes where and when. On Friday morning, the trainee told the PHG that he was a bit worried about next week. The PHG told him not to worry as, by the time he went home at lunchtime on Saturday, he'd have learned enough to do the job. The trainee then told the PHG that he wasn't worried about whether he would actually have grasped enough to be able to do the job. He was just worried that he, the trainee, was scheduled to be on holiday next week too. Does the phrase 'piss up in a brewery' come to mind?

MAD WORLD 75
OUTLAWS COME TO LUNCH AGAIN

Day off work, whopping headache and the Outlaws are coming to lunch.
 What could possibly go wrong?
 I don't know about you, perhaps I'm biased, but I always thought the best thing about Outlaws, that is to say Jayne's parents, was that they only have to come to lunch once a year around Christmas/ New Year and then you can relax for another twelve months. But, following Jayne's Mum having a knee operation, Jayne thought we should extend a one-off invite to her parents to join us for Sunday dinner. Maybe that's why I awoke with a whopping headache. It was stress induced after all.
 Things were going as well as expected as I chomped quietly on my roast potatoes. The Outlaws were in full swing on the subject of Jayne's younger brother. He has a remarkable knack of marrying young ladies and then having a couple of kids as fast as he can before the divorce. The recent escapade has reached the mudslinging in court stage where the younger brother stands in one corner in a suit and tie while the aggrieved (?) opponent stands in the opposite corner next to the broom stick she just arrived on. I've experienced more than my fair share of this particular sport in my own family. As my stomach was getting nicely filled with roast potatoes, I reached a point where I'd had a belly full of this tale of the younger brother's woes. So I decided to lighten the mood.
 "Jayne," I said, "I bet if you had ever phoned your Mum in the last 20 years to tell her that you had split with Steve,

your Mum would have jumped up and down and clapped her hands with glee."
   Nobody laughed.
      Silence.
   Should that tell me something?

MAD WORLD 76
LIGHTBULB MOMENT

Three things happened recently that made me smile. I would like to share them with you today.

I was moving some motorbikes around on the drive at home when a young lady we know stopped for a chat on her way home from school. She is twelve years old and can be quite fun to talk to. She suddenly said: "Steve, you see that number plate on your bike?"

"Which one?" I replied.

"The one that says PGL xxx R."

"What about it?" I asked.

Her answer caught me by surprise: "Parents Get Lost."

I was delivering to a very good friend of mine one morning who I see daily whether I have anything for her or not. The lady is wheelchair bound but seems to enjoy my daily visits as much as I do. The good-humored banter has lasted for many years and long may it continue. She has agreed to the retelling of this particular piece of fun.

I delivered an envelope containing an appointment at the Hospital to see the dentist. Any appointment at the Hospital results in at least half a day out by Ambulance with the preparations beforehand starting in the early hours with the help of several of the troops and planning worthy of a military operation. She uses a hoist to get in and out of bed. My good friend told me how she needed to see the dentist to have a broken front tooth repaired. She always tells the dentist that if the work they are going to do will be less painful than having a baby then she won't have an injection. I just had to ask the question: "Do you have a male dentist or a female dentist?"

"It's a man." came the reply.
"Then how on earth would a man know how painful it is to have a baby?"

Twenty years ago, my employer hired staff who were intelligent, dedicated, conscientious, witty, and modest. But maybe I'm biased. These days they seem to have an 'any numpty will do' approach.

A colleague of mine was parking his car at 4.30 am in the car park before work. Another colleague told him that his car had only one reversing light working. Later that day, the colleague with the car rang his garage to book it in to have the bulb changed. That could be the cue for a 'how many of my colleagues does it take to change a light bulb?' joke but these short stories have to be kept down to 500 words. When the day came for the trip to the garage, my colleague duly went along but was told the mechanic was out on a breakdown. So, my colleague decided to wait. Half an hour later the mechanic returned to the garage and, after apologizing for keeping the customer waiting, asked what the problem was with the car?

"My car only has one reversing light." my colleague told the mechanic.

"That's right," said the mechanic, "VW Polos only have one reversing light."

MAD WORLD 77
CHURCH OR PUB?

At long last, I now have a story to tell. Here are a couple of highlights from the wedding job I did on Saturday. Boy, wasn't it hot? No air conditioning in the Rolls and I was gone 6 hours in total and covered just over 100 miles.

The bride and the bride's father came out of the house and the bride told her father to slam the front door shut as she had a key. With the both of them safely loaded into the Rolls, I was all set for the 30 minutes trip with the bride wanting to arrive at the Church at 2.20pm. It was now 10 to 2. So, all set then? Bride shouts: "Oh no, my bouquet is indoors." The father asks for the key and she says she hasn't actually got it with her as it has gone on ahead with all her other stuff. So, he tries a couple of other questions. "Key with the neighbour?" No. "Shall we break in?" No. After lots of comforting noises and the suggestion that a bouquet from one of the bridesmaids would have to suffice, we set off down the tiny country lanes to get to the church. We now had to do the 30 minutes trip in 25 minutes. But I managed it. As we drove into the village we had to drive around a bend to park by the main entrance to the church. Straight in front of us, before going around the bend, is the pub with tables and chairs set up outside where all the guests who should have been sitting in the church by now were sitting at the tables having a pint or two. And judging by the panic now erupting in the back of my car, I think the groom may have been spotted sitting there sipping a pint as well. "Drive on, drive on." Came the shout from the back seat. And I thought these things only ever happen on the television. We had to go up the road and turn around while all the guests legged it up the road to the church. Four bridesmaids were at the church so two of them gave the bride their flowers so that two of them with flowers and two of them without would look OK. Good move. The church service was completed in 30 minutes. Can't believe they actually covered everything in 30 minutes but there you go. So, they all piled out of the church and, after one or two photos, the groom announces that they aren't allowed to arrive at the reception until 4 pm and as they appear to be a bit early, "Why don't we all go back to the pub?" All the guests, the bride and groom and the photographer march off down the lane to the pub. You really couldn't make this stuff up if you tried.

MAD WORLD 78
VIRUS OR INFECTION?

Sorry I'm missing from the village at the moment. I would say it seems a regular thing for this to happen each winter but it seems to happen in the summer as well. But I shall return.

In my absence, no doubt my employer will have implemented their 'get to meet your neighbour' initiative before it is rolled out nationally. The idea, as many of you already know, is that you get the chance to visit your neighbour to give them their letters and, if you're lucky, they'll give you some of your own. This way of delivering letters is a far more efficient way of doing it as it means my relief colleagues don't have to waste valuable time reading the addresses on the envelopes.

Anyway, after a few days off work, I decided to take my virus along to show my doctor as I felt sure he probably hadn't seen one as good as mine before. But my doctor was off sick trying one out for himself. I had to agree to see another doctor. I've always been wary of some of these alternative medical methods but agreed to try one on this occasion. I didn't know if it was going to be a man or a woman doctor though. However, judging by the surname, I guessed that the doctor might not be the same nationality as me. When I walked in, I discovered it to be a large lady with a nut and bolt through her nose. Gee whiz. Why do people do that to their bodies? I shall never understand why anyone wants to put additional holes in their body. I have my hands full coping with those that I've had since birth. I sure as heck don't need any more. I had my opening line ready. It was going to be along the lines of, 'It's OK for you because you've got me, but I've only got you.' But I bottled it half way through. I managed "My usual doctor is off sick so I'm afraid you've got me," which was probably nearer the truth anyway. Well, she told me she had had what I had got, 3 times. No, she didn't tell me 3 times. She had had it 3 times! Wow. What a fantastic surgery. The doctors try out all the illnesses before the patients get them so then they know what's wrong with you before you do. I went in with what I thought was a virus and came out with an infection.

MAD WORLD 79
EXPENSIVE LOAF

Here we go again. Twice in one week? I think you need to bear in mind the pressure Jayne and I work under at this time of year, Christmas, which could explain our odd sense of humour. But this did make us laugh even though we shouldn't have.

At the beginning of December, Jayne was invited to display, and hopefully sell, some of her concrete creations and knitted creations at the village WI table-top sale. They had been so impressed with Jayne's stall the previous year that they invited her back. With a few new lines added to the range and a few plants from the one man band Post Office at Ninfield to help make a display, everything was set. Jayne's Mum was enlisted to help man the stall and there were a good few friends and relatives set to come along on the day including Jayne's Dad and his brother, Jayne's uncle, who lives on his own. One of the other tables at the table-top sale was a local baker. Uncle splashed out about £1.60 on one of their bread loaves although he did notice it was a bit hard. Now for the bit that made us laugh. Yes, perhaps we should get out more. Uncle, when back home, cut a slice of the nice local bread and bit into it, broke a tooth, went to the dentist, had it repaired and got a bill for £260.00. Not bad for a £1.60 loaf.

MAD WORLD 80
VITAMIN 'C'

Well not so much a Mad World perhaps but more of the life and times of. But then again, that always has been a Mad World.

Vitamin C is good for you, or so the lady who has kept me supplied with the tablets for years always said. But not good for the teeth it would appear. On Tuesday morning, there I was, about to walk out the door at 5 am to go to work and after popping two vitamin C tablets into my mouth, I felt an uncharacteristic crunch and out popped a tooth. Sheared clean off. Jayne was not impressed that I had left the tooth on the side in the kitchen while I contemplated what to do next during the course of the morning. I've had good results in the past dealing with sharp teeth or broken teeth with a good nail file, a torch and a mirror but have no experience of dealing with craters.

On Tuesday afternoon, I popped into the dentist and showed the tooth to the chap in reception. He also wasn't impressed and made me an appointment for Wednesday afternoon. So, there I was the following afternoon, sitting in the dentist's chair and the lady dentist stuck her head in my mouth and had a look around. It seemed to echo when she called out: "It's a big TOOOOTH." I couldn't help thinking the word, 'was', should have appeared somewhere in that sentence. When she came back out of my mouth, I got the tooth out of my pocket to show her. She too wasn't impressed. I could see a pattern emerging here. I had spent the best part of 50 years being very impressed with that tooth and now, suddenly, no one was very impressed with it at all. Not even me. The dentist gave me two options:

1. I could have the remainder of the tooth extracted. I had a really bad experience about ten years ago having a tooth extracted by a previous dentist. On that occasion, I ended up needing a course of antibiotics and a long lie down. I remember thinking at the time that this particular dentist must have learned his trade working in the Foreign Legion. But of course, my concerns were dismissed at home and I was considered to be making an awful lot of fuss over just having a tooth out. However, several months later we read in the local paper that the dentist had been struck off. His knack of pinning little old ladies down with his knee while taking their teeth out had never really caught on and several of the little old ladies had ganged up on him and got their own back.

2. I could have what was left of the tooth capped. This would involve several appointments, lots of money (about £250) and, as the root had already been worked on in the past, all of that work would have to be dug out and then she would have to go in even deeper. Even deeper? I had visions of the drill bit coming out of the top of my head. "And" the dentist went on, "there would only be a 70% chance of success." I told the dentist I hadn't heard an option I liked the sound of yet. So could she please continue? "There is the option of just filling the tooth, or what's left of it." But she wouldn't recommend that. "Why not?" I asked. "Because there is no guarantee how long it would last." She told me. I suggested there didn't appear to be any convincing guarantee with the £250 option she had been telling me about.

So, I now have a temporary filling in place until I go back for my regular check up in a couple of weeks. Then I must give her my decision. But I've already told her I will probably come back and just have it filled.

Other work related news. On Easter Saturday, on returning to the office, I suggested my van, a Vauxhall

Combi, really should be looked at by a garage. The transmission was very noisy. So, on the Tuesday morning my van was taken away, apparently needing a new gearbox and I was given another van to use for the week. A Fiat Diabolical. By Friday, the Fiat Diabolical had had enough of driving around the bumpy tracks in the village and as I was driving up to a farm, the cam belt snapped which could have destroyed the engine. I tried phoning the office on my mobile phone but most mobile phones don't work very well in the village. You either get a poor signal or no signal at all. When the office phone was answered, the two of us then began the hopeless, "Hello, hello, hello, hello," fiasco. As I could already see another late finish looming, I began to lose my cool. I shouted down the phone in despair: "You're supposed to hold the phone to your ear, not your backside." "Oh, hello Steve, I can hear you now." So now you'll see me in a very nice V W Caddy van. A hire van. We have about 8 or 9 hire vans spread across our 2 offices. But the drawback is, they don't fit down our alley way. So we have to try and find a space every afternoon in the free bit of the car park in the Mount Street car park. Such fun at the end of the working day.

MAD WORLD 81 PRIVATIZATION. STUCK IN REVERSE

I know it's Donkeys Yonks' since I last wrote but I think maybe it's time for me to at least try and see a funny side to the great privatization con before I go on strike in a couple of weeks. Mind you, the first strike that has been announced is on a Monday which is my day off, so I shall just have to pretend to be on strike. A little old lady went up to the counter in our local Post Office the other day and asked Jayne: "Can I still trust you now that you have been privatized?"

"I haven't been privatized," Jayne replied. "Oh yes you have," said the lady. "Oh no I haven't," replied Jayne. "Where have you been?" The lady went on, "it's been in all the newspapers and on the television that Royal Mail has been privatized."

"But I'm not Royal Mail," Jayne told her.

"Aren't You?" Asked the lady. "No, we are the Post Office," Jayne said. "But you have got your shares?" The lady queried. "Oh no, I haven't," said Jayne. "The postmen are getting shares, but they haven't got them yet either. But we aren't getting any shares because we aren't anything to do with Royal Mail." "Oh", said the lady, "so I can still trust you then?" They really don't have a clue, do they? It reminded me of a time about 20 years ago when a chap on my round asked me to tell someone when I got back to the office that his phone wasn't working. Well, I did tell someone but what good that was meant to do I shall never know.

Changing the subject. As some of you already know, I've been driving some brilliant hire vans since Easter. Much better than anything my employer will ever buy. Much better for my back for getting in and out of. About 3 weeks ago, I was given another V W Caddy van to use. Only done 120 miles so practically brand new. Up to the end of last week it had got up to around 800 miles on the clock. On Monday this week, my day off, a colleague used it to do my delivery and jammed the gearbox when selecting 1st gear at a junction. On the V W Caddy vans, reverse is next to 1st on the gear stick. I prefer reverse to be over the other side below 5th on the gear stick. Out of harm's way. A recovery lorry was called for and it was a brand-new lorry. The recovery man had to connect his winch to the rear of the van so as to then winch it up the ramp on to his low loader. Recovery chaps always have the steering unlocked when winching vehicles on to their lorry as it would be hopeless trying to winch a vehicle on if the steering kept locking. On the V W Caddy van, I have noticed that to unlock the steering column you have to have the ignition turned on. Yes, you really do. As the Caddy van was being winched backwards up the ramp the front wheels reached the bottom of the ramp and the engine fired. It had effectively bump started itself. It was now apparent that the gear that the gearbox was jammed in was reverse. The recovery man had no option but to jump out of the way as the V W Caddy van came along his low loader and smacked in to the cab of his nice new lorry before falling off the side of the lorry and ending up in the bushes. I bet that took some explaining to his boss. As an office, we have scrapped 6 vans this year with another 2 under assessment. Now the recovery chaps are helping us add to the total.

MAD WORLD 82
POLLING DAY

Jayne took part in the recent vote for the new Police Commissioner. Jayne had a 15 hour stint in the polling station with several colleagues checking each voter as they came in to the local church hall. It was like spot the voter, unfortunately, as the 15 hour opening time only produced 119 people who were interested enough to vote.

For those of you who didn't make it to your local polling station for the election for Police Commissioner, the voting slip has two columns so a voter has to select their first choice of candidate in column one and their second choice of candidate in column two. Of course, next month we have the 'stay in or come out', vote for the European Referendum to see if anyone actually wants to keep sending obscene amounts of our money abroad. The clue there is, of course, it will be an in or out vote.

Fairly late in the day on Thursday, Jayne and her colleagues were pleased to see yet another voter keen to place their 'X' on a voting slip to elect the Police Commissioner for Sussex. The voter toddled up to where Jayne and her colleagues were sitting and the polling card was handed over to Jayne who was the first polling clerk. Then the name was ticked off on the electoral roll by the second polling clerk as the third polling clerk explained the procedure with the voting slip.

"There are 2 columns on the voting slip, column 1 is for your first choice of candidate and column 2 is for your second choice of candidate." said the polling clerk.

Just as the 3 clerks were thinking the information had gone in and been understood, a question came back.

"Will I have to put down 2 choices for the Euro vote next month?"

Unfortunately, Jayne slowly sank beneath the table in a fit of hysterical laughter.

I haven't written any Mad World stuff for about 10 years, but with my book writing on hold until after Christmas, I thought I might share this with you. Blame Tina for asking me the question: what was the acupuncture like? But a Mad World from me can't be any worse than watching the national news at the moment, can it?

MAD WORLD 83
ACUPUNCTURE. AND DOGS

I had my first ever acupuncture appointment yesterday. This was for my Plantar Fasciitis (Policeman's Heel) problem. Left foot, heel has hurt ever since I did a dog walk about 5 months ago on the Downs at Butts Brow. I was wearing an old pair of work boots back then as my new walking boots had only just arrived and I didn't want to risk wearing them for an hour or more straight out of the box. Big mistake. Blisters would have been easier to deal with. So, in an effort to try something new to see if it might help the problem, I booked in for an acupuncture session.

The nice lady, after making all kinds of notes about my bodily problems over the years and hearing about how I damaged my heel dog walking, had me lying face down on the bench in my underpants. After pressing her thumb in to various parts of my heel, she found the most painful bit and proceeded to stick a needle in it. Holy Smoke! I nearly went through the roof. My other leg shot up and I told her to make sure she stays well clear of my other leg because if she's going to be doing any more of that she might get kicked. She assured me that she was standing well clear of my other leg and continued inserting needles, some of which were more painful than others. The lady decided to make conversation whilst treating me and asked: "How long have you been a dog lover?" What a stupid question to ask me. Unfortunately, my immediate reaction was somewhat animated and she had to shout "Careful, you've got needles in." What did she expect? I tried to explain that I have never been a dog lover, only do dog walking to help Jayne and the best bit of any dog walk is when it's over. On the occasion when I hurt my heel, I had been dog walking on my own and had a lot on my mind as it was about then that my doctor had told me I wouldn't be going back to work and I was no doubt walking too fast as I was nearly back at my car.

So, with that ordeal out of the way and another session organised for January, we come to last night. Jayne had bags under her eyes last night so I decided that I would get up to do the boys during the night. We went to bed about 9 pm and I waited. About 10.30, the barking/shouting started. There must have been a fox passing by about 5 miles away that Bentley thought I needed to know about. I got out of bed, went in to the kitchen and gave Bentley an almighty telling off at the top of my voice and smacked him on the nose. Bentley enjoys winding me up. So he wagged his tail. "Don't you wag your tail when I am telling you off," I told him, smacked his nose again and slammed the door on the way out.

I got back into bed and waited. About 1 am, the barking started again. The fox must have been on his way back. This time, both Bentley and Royce were out of bed when I opened the kitchen door. They took one look at me and I can honestly say I have never seen them get back into their beds so fast. I hadn't even said a word. I mixed some tablets up for my headache and pointed out to them that I had already got them banned from the bedroom and they would be finding a few other things will be changing from now on. We didn't get any more noise until Jayne got up about 6 o'clock.

I got up about 9 o'clock feeling like death warmed up. Jayne asked me how I was. I told Jayne I would be fine once we get rid of those dogs.

Full credit to Jayne, she went away and thought about it. Then came back and told me that a friend of hers who now lives in a guest house had been worried about her dogs barking at night and disturbing the guests. So she had fitted special collars to her dogs and they are quiet all night. Jayne went on to say that she had never approved of the idea of fitting collars that give any kind of electrical shock to a dog (sounds like a fantastic idea to me, where do we get those?) and that her friend had assured Jayne that the collars she uses don't give electric shocks. Oh, what a shame.

I told Jayne that if the collars work and the dogs stay quiet all night, I would be able to fit the new collars each day after a dog walk because it would then be like they weren't here at all and that would be paradise. I got told off for that idea.

Jayne has sent a message to her friend to find out how to get some of those collars. I told Jayne that I couldn't give a toss what anyone might think as it had to be better than me going for acupuncture next month and being asked: "So what made you buy a shotgun?"

MAD WORLD 84
HELP YOURSELF

Some very good friends of ours decided they would like to declutter their house and garage. However, they didn't want to hold a garage sale or throw stuff away. They came up with the idea of putting a big box at the bottom of their drive full of the things they no longer wanted to keep. Beside the box they had put a handwritten sign saying, 'Please Help Yourself.'

That was quite successful so, several months later, they decided to have another go. This time they thought they would improve the presentation of the items they were giving away. So they put a table at the bottom of their drive and displayed their wares on the table. The same sign was put up, 'Please Help Yourself'. The first day went well so they did the same the following day. Later that day they checked their display to see how things were going. Very well it would seem. Someone had pulled all the goods on to the ground and taken the table. That was the only thing they had wanted to keep.

Printed in Great Britain
by Amazon